The Voices of Toni Morrison

The
Voices
of Toni
Morrison

Barbara Hill Rigney

Ohio State University Press
Columbus

Library of Congress Cataloging-in-Publication Data

Rigney, Barbara Hill, 1938–
    The voices of Toni Morrison / Barbara Hill Rigney.
      p. cm.
    Includes bibliographical references and index.
    ISBN 0–8142–0554–2 (alk. paper)
    1. Morrison, Toni—Criticism and interpretation. 2. Feminism and
literature—United States—History—20th century. 3. Afro-American
women in literature. I. Title.
PS3563.O8749Z84 1991
813'.54—dc20   91–16092
                                                CIP

Text and jacket design by Hunter Graphics.
Type set in ITC Galliard by G&S Typesetters, Austin, TX.
Printed by Bookcrafters, Chelsea, MI.

The paper in this book meets the guidelines for permanence and durability of the
Committee on Production Guidelines for Book Longevity of the Council on
Library Resources. ∞

Printed in the U.S.A.

9 8 7 6 5 4 3 2 1

For Kim, Julie, Kris, Sky, and Papa

I gratefully acknowledge the time and the encouragement provided by the College of Humanities and the Department of English at The Ohio State University, the support of my editor, Charlotte Dihoff, and the invaluable assistance and advice of both colleagues and students, most particularly Murray Beja, Erika Bourguignon, Grace Epstein, Michael Hitt, Sebastian Knowles, Marlene Longenecker, and James Phelan.

Contents

Introduction

> . . . what is important is to disconcert the staging of represen-
> tation according to *exclusively* "masculine" parameters, that is,
> according to phallocratic order. It is not a matter of toppling
> that order so as to replace it—that amounts to the same thing
> in the end—but of disrupting and modifying it, starting from
> an "outside" that is exempt, in part, from phallocratic law.
> —Irigaray, *This Sex Which Is Not One*

From her vantage at the intersection of race and gender, Toni Morrison represents an exemption from "phallocratic law"; her own language and her theory of language, as she has demonstrated in her five novels and explained in a number of essays and interviews, reflect a consciousness that she writes both from and about a zone that is "outside" of literary convention, that disrupts traditional Western ideological confines and modifies patriarchal inscriptions. While no American writer, regardless of race or gender, can be considered as totally outside of the dominant signifying structure, there is nonetheless an area on the periphery, a zone both chosen and allocated, which represents a way of seeing and of knowing that disconcerts and finally discounts the very structure which excludes it. Mapping that zone as Morrison delineates it most radically—through language, through a rendering of history, through a reinscription of identity, and through the articulation of female desire—is the concern of the following study, which seeks to place Morrison's works within the context of a black feminine/feminist aesthetic and to define that aesthetic in terms of contemporary feminist and African American critical theory.

According to French feminist theorists Hélène Cixous and Catherine Clément in *The Newly Born Woman*: "It is impossible to *define* a feminist practice of writing, and this is an impossibility that will remain, for this practice can never be theorized, enclosed, coded—which doesn't mean that it doesn't exist. . . . It will be conceived of only by subjects who are breakers of automatisms,

1

by peripheral figures that no authority can ever subjugate" (313). Morrison is surely one of these "peripheral figures" in terms of the dominant culture, central though she is to the contemporary literary scene. For Morrison—as is also true for many other contemporary African American women writers, including Alice Walker, Toni Cade Bambara, and Gloria Naylor, to name three—gender is not separate or separable from racial identity; while their arguments are for liberation from racial and gender oppression, both race and gender themselves are always seen as liberating points from which to construct a language or to create a literature that is political in form as well as in subject matter. As Morrison consciously writes the black text, so she also defines herself as "valuable as a writer because I am a woman, because women, it seems to me, have some special knowledge about certain things. [It comes from] the ways in which they view the world and from women's imagination. Once it is unruly and let loose it can bring things to the surface that men—trained to be men in a certain way—have difficulty getting access to" (Lester, 54).

In Morrison's texts, to be "other," i.e., black and female, is to have privileged insights, access to that "special knowledge" she both inscribes and describes repeatedly in her novels. In keeping with the paradox that is also her fictional text, Morrison celebrates "otherness" but simultaneously also resists participation in what art sections of the popular press are currently calling "artistic tribalism" and "the cult of otherness." Morrison has said of African Americans: "We are not, in fact, 'other.' We are choices. And to read imaginative literature by and about us is to choose to examine centers of the self and to have the opportunity to compare these centers with the 'raceless' one with which we are, all of us, most familiar" (1990, 208). She writes, finally, she says, about that which "has something to do with life and being human in the world" (Tate 1989, 121). Perhaps, as Morrison illustrates, it is possible to be both "other" and "human in the world" without, at the same time, serving the gods of traditional Western humanism.

For Morrison's fictions *do* represent otherness, in which fact lies their great strength, for from her very marginality she presents a mirror to the larger culture as well as to the African American culture, and the image contained there is often a revelation. For Morrison, to recognize the other as one's "self," to come to terms with one's own otherness, to enter willingly the forbidden zones of consciousness (and unconsciousness) that lie through and beyond the mirror of gender and race, is to become more fully human, more moral, and more sane. Often Morrison presents this psychic zone in terms that emphasize rather than minimize its cultural otherness, for she guides her reader through metaphoric jungles, through representations of the conjure world,[1] and through images of an Africa of the mind that is repressed but never totally lost or forgotten, a part of the unconscious which surfaces in racial memory, particularly for African Americans.

Perhaps Elaine Showalter is generally correct in her argument that the anthropologically defined "wild zone"[2] of female space within the literary text is, at least for most women writers, a "playful abstraction: in the reality to which we must address ourselves as critics, women's writing is a 'double-voiced discourse' that always embodies the social, literary, and cultural heritages of both the muted and the dominant" (1985, 263). But Morrison invites her own inclusion into a very much less abstract and not always so playful wild zone, a place where women's imagination is "unruly and let loose," as she herself describes it, and where language is subversive, where the female body claims the power to articulate itself, where silence speaks and the unconscious becomes the conscious.

Largely outside the myth of American homogeneity, freer than most American theorists of the thumbprint of patriarchal discourse in spite of their acknowledged debts to such theorists as Derrida, Lacan, and Foucault, the French feminist theorists are those who most pointedly seek to investigate the feminine language, who have begun to map the "wild zone," and who might provide a metaphoric structure by which to approach the nature of Morrison's marginality and her difference. For Morrison does write what the French call *différence*, that feminine style that opens the closure of binary oppositions and thus subverts many of the basic assumptions of Western humanistic thought. The important metaphor that pervades the works of such theorists as Luce Irigaray, Julia Kristeva, Hélène Cixous, Catherine Clément, Marguerite Duras, and Monique Wittig, is in fact that of marginality, of blackness as symbolic of radical dissidence and linguistic revolution. Duras, for example, defines feminine writing as "an organic translated writing . . . translated from blackness, from darkness . . . from the unknown, like a new way of communicating rather than an already formed language" (quoted by Marks, 174). Cixous, too, in "The Laugh of the Medusa," aligns herself with all women, whom she perceives as victimized by but victorious over white patriarchy: "We the precocious, we the repressed of culture, our lovely mouths gagged with pollen, our wind knocked out of us, we the labyrinths, the ladders, the trampled spaces . . . we are black and we are beautiful" (310). Women, write Cixous and Clément in *The Newly Born Woman*, are "the Dark Continent" (68). "Blackness" as metaphor, for Morrison as well as for these French theorists, embraces racial identity *and* a state of female consciousness, or even unconsciousness, that zone beyond the laws of white patriarchy in which female art is conceived and produced.

Ann Rosalind Jones sees many aspects of French feminisms as limited in political application, the constitution of "an energizing myth" (372) rather than an agenda for change, but she also defends the works of French feminists as "an island of hope in the void left by the deconstruction of humanism"; they represent "a powerful alternative discourse . . . to write from the body is to re-create the world" (366). The following study also frequently employs the language of contemporary French feminists when that becomes useful—not as a defense or even as an analysis of their works, certainly not as a limiting construct on Morrison's own politically and artistically powerful voice, but as "an island of hope," as an alternative discourse, a radical way to approach the radical aspects of Morrison's fictions, a means of interpreting and translating the double-voiced discourse which is Morrison's text. Like the powerful Eva in *Sula*, Morrison herself speaks "with two voices. Like two people were talking at the same time, saying the same thing, one a fraction of a second behind the other" (61).

Feminist scholars of African American literature are also fully aware of the philosophical two-step necessary to approach the double voices of writers like Morrison, and it is they, most specifically, who warn of the dangers involved in subsuming racial difference into the category of the feminine. Some scholars have expressed their concern that all theory as practiced in the academy today is largely inappropriate for the interpretation of African American literature in general. Barbara Christian, in "The Race for Theory," for example, sees critical theory as "hegemonic as the world it attacks. I see the language it creates as one that mystifies rather than clarifies our condition, making it possible for a few people who know that particular language to control the critical scene" (1988, 71). Morrison herself has questioned the validity of the application of traditional critical paradigms to African American texts, suggesting that they may "constitute a disguise for a temporal, political and culturally specific program" (1990, 202). Even within the context of her fiction, Morrison extends a subtle warning about the nature and relevance of critical scholarship as applied to her work. In her earliest novel, *The Bluest Eye*, she depicts Elihue Micah Whitcomb, alias Soaphead Church, who advertises himself as "Reader, Adviser, and Interpreter of Dreams" (130), and who comes from "a family proud of its academic accomplishments and its mixed blood" (132):

> Little Elihue learned everything he needed to know well, particularly the fine art of self-deception. He read greedily but understood selectively, choosing the bits and pieces of other men's ideas that supported whatever predilection he had at the moment. Thus he chose to remember Hamlet's abuse of Ophelia, but not Christ's love of Mary Magdalene; Hamlet's frivolous politics, but not Christ's serious anarchy. . . . For all his exposure to the best minds of the Western world, he allowed only the narrowest interpretation to touch him. . . . A hatred of, and fascination with, any hint of disorder or decay. (133–34)

As the following chapters will attempt to document, Morrison's own fictions include more than a bit of controlled disorder and a great deal of serious anarchy, and these are aspects any scholar must consider despite her or his own self-deceptions and predilections, from which none of us is totally free.

The criteria necessary for the "sane accountability" in the consideration of texts by African American women that Barbara Smith requests in "Toward a Black Feminist Criticism" (1985, 183) involves a refusal to separate categories like race and gender, to view a writer like Morrison in the context of "both/and" rather than "either/or," and to perform, as Beloved does, "A little two-step, two-step, make-a-new-step, slide, slide and strut on down" (*Beloved*, 74). The following study seeks to represent that new-step, which is the cultivation of a common ground for theory, race, and gender.

1

Breaking the Back of Words: Language and Signification

> The most valuable point of entry into the question of cultural (or racial) distinction, the one most fraught, is its language—its unpoliced, seditious, confrontational, manipulative, inventive, disruptive, masked and unmasking language.
> —Morrison, 1990, "Unspeakable Things Unspoken"

A consideration of language is primary in the development of theoretical paradigms as these relate to all literatures, but particularly to the African American feminine/feminist text. This is especially true in a critical approach to Toni Morrison's works, for, like the Sibyl of mythology, Morrison scatters her signs, her political insights, and it is only through an analysis of her language that we can reconstruct an idea of the political and artistic revolution constituted in her work. "Confrontational," "unpoliced," hers is the language of black and feminine discourse—semiotic, maternal, informed as much by silence as by dialogue, as much by absence as by presence. Morrison seems to *conjure* her language, to invent a form of discourse that is always at once both metaphysical and metafictional.

One of the freedoms Morrison claims in her novels is to move beyond language, even while working *through* it, to incorporate significance beyond the denotation of words, to render experience and emotion, for example, as musicians do. Morrison says that she wishes to accomplish "something that has probably only been fully expressed in music. . . . Writing novels is a way to encompass this—this something" (McKay, 1). The enigma of freedom itself,

7

to be discovered at the margins of the dominant culture, can best be expressed, Morrison writes, through the analogy, even through an imitation, of music:

> The pieces of Cholly's life could become coherent only in the head of a musician. Only those who talk their talk through the gold of curved metal, or in the touch of black-and-white rectangles and taut skins and strings echoing from wooden corridors, could give true form to his life . . . and come up with all of what that meant in joy, in pain, in anger, in love, and give it its final and pervading ache of freedom. Only a musician would sense, know, without even knowing that he knew, that Cholly was free. Dangerously free. (*The Bluest Eye*, 125)

Like the blues-singing women who populate her fiction, like the prostitute Poland in her "sweet strawberry voice" (*The Bluest Eye*, 49), or like Claudia's mother who can sing "misery colored by greens and blues" and make pain sweet (*The Bluest Eye*, 24), so Morrison also sings her novels (and anyone who has heard Morrison read from her work will know this is literally as well as metaphorically true). Images of music pervade her work, but so also does a musical quality of language, a sound and rhythm that permeate and radiate in every novel.

Pilate, for example, "sings" throughout *Song of Solomon*, in which both the motif of music and the musicality of language are so crucial. The solution to Milkman's quest is found in the words and the rhythms of a song, the same song his aunt Pilate sings on the first page of the novel, and his rediscovered grandmother is significantly named "Sing Byrd." The duet sung by Pilate and Reba at Hagar's funeral is spontaneous, yet staged, theatrical, an operatic performance, typical of the way these particular women have always communicated among themselves. All Pilate's words are musical, rhythmic, as the young Milkman realizes: "Her voice made Milkman think of pebbles. Little round pebbles that bumped up against each other. Maybe she was hoarse, or maybe it was the way she said her words, with both a drawl and a clip" (40).

And if *Beloved* is not, as Morrison writes, "a story to pass on" (274), then it is certainly one to be sung. Morrison describes "the sound of the novel, sometimes cacophonous, sometimes harmonious, [which] must be an inner ear sound or a sound just beyond hearing, infusing the text with a musical emphasis that words can do sometimes even better than music can" (1990, 228). Sethe often recounts her "rememories" in the form of songs, made-up ballads for her children, which constitute a transmission of history and of culture, but it is also her conversation, even her thoughts, which are musical. Beloved's own voice is "gravelly" with "a song that seemed to lie in it. Just outside music it lay, with a cadence not like theirs" (60). All women's songs, Morrison indicates, are "just outside music"; often also they are codes, ways to break an enforced silence; they constitute a protest. Cixous writes, in "The Laugh of the Medusa," "In women's speech, and in their writing, that element which never stops resonating, which, once we've been permeated by it, profoundly and imperceptibly touched by it, retains the power of moving us—that element is the song: first music from the first voice of love which is alive in every woman" (312). And also in Morrison's terms, music and the singing of women have a power beyond words, a transcendent meaning that can provide "the right combination, the key, the code, the sound that broke the back of words . . . a wave of sound wide enough to sound deep water and knock the pods off chestnut trees" (*Beloved*, 261).

Certain men, too, are permitted the expression of song in Morrison's fiction. Milkman, who, in addition to his other failings, "knew no songs, and had no singing voice" (*Song of Solomon*, 340), learns to sing only on the last page of the novel when, at Pilate's request, he sings loud enough to wake the birds, although not the dying Pilate. Sixo, in *Beloved*, who needs no Pilate because suffering has been his teacher, confronts death with his hand on the mouth of a rifle and singing a song; it is the song which tells the white captor that Sixo is free in his soul and that he cannot be taken alive. All the songs at Sweet Home are expressions of a desire for freedom in which "yearning fashioned every note" (40). In Alfred, Georgia, Paul D sings his passion in songs that are "flat-headed nails for pounding and pounding and pounding" (40). Dancing "two-step to the music of hand-forged iron," Paul D and the other chained convicts

> sang it out and beat it up, garbling the words so they could not
> be understood; tricking the words so their syllables yielded up
> other meanings. They sang the women they knew; the children
> they had been; the animals they had tamed themselves or seen

others tame. They sang of bosses and masters and misses; of
mules and dogs and the shamelessness of life. They sang lov-
ingly of graveyards and sisters long gone. . . . Singing love
songs to Mr. Death, they smashed his head. More than the rest,
they killed the flirt whom folks called Life for leading them on.
Making them think the next sunrise would be worth it; that
another stroke of time would do it at last. (108–9)

These songs, like those sung by women, are subversive, "garbled
so they could not be understood," and they speak the lost language of Africa, the language of Sethe's mother "which would
never come back" (62), and a heritage of freedom.

Like music, but even less intelligible, far more mystical, is
Morrison's recurrent evocation of a sound that transcends language, a primal cry that echoes from prehistory and also breaks
"the back of words." The Word of the father and even of God is
rewritten by the women of *Beloved*, who know that "In the beginning there were no words. In the beginning was the sound, and
they all knew what that sounded like" (259). As we also learn in
Song of Solomon along with Milkman, this metaphysical sound,
this transcendence of language, is

what there was before language. Before things were written
down. Language in the time when men and animals did talk to
one another, when a man could sit down with an ape and the
two converse; when a tiger and a man could share the same tree,
and each understood the other; when men ran *with* wolves, not
from or after them. And he was hearing it in the Blue Ridge
Mountains under a sweet gum tree. And if they could talk to
animals, and the animals could talk to them, what didn't they
know about human beings? Or the earth itself. . . . (281)

What Milkman hears here and from Pilate, what Sethe echoes, is
the "mother tongue," which, according to Kristeva, is "beyond
and within, more or less than meaning: rhythm, tone, color, and
joy, within, through, and across the Word" (1980, 158).

Karla Holloway and Stephanie Demetrokopoulos write in
New Dimensions of Spirituality that "Black women carry the voice
of the mother—they are the progenitors. . . . Women, as carriers
of the *voice*, carry wisdom—mother wit" (123). Throughout
Morrison's novels, women are the primary tale-tellers and the
transmitters of history as well as the singing teachers; only they

know the language of the occult and the occult of language and thus comprise what Morrison has called a "feminine subtext" (1990, 220). In *The Bluest Eye*, Claudia and her sister Frieda are spellbound by the rhythmic conversation of women, the sound of which is more important than the sense, moving far beyond language and even beyond music:

> Their conversation is like a gently wicked dance: sound meets sound, curtsies, shimmies, and retires. Another sound enters but is upstaged by still another: the two circle each other and stop. Sometimes their words move in lofty spirals; other times they take strident leaps, and all of it is punctuated with warm-pulsed laughter—like the throb of a heart made of jelly. The edge, the curl, the thrust of their emotions is always clear to Frieda and me. We do not, cannot, know the meanings of all their words, for we are nine and ten years old. So we watch their faces, their hands, their feet, and listen for truth in timbre. (16)

Perhaps it is the fluidity, the *jouissance*, in black women's speech that is so musical, so erotic, and that accomplishes "truth in timbre." Again in *The Bluest Eye*, Morrison not only describes but recreates the effect of musical language:

> They come from Mobile. Aiken. From Newport News. From Marietta. From Meridian. And the sounds of these places in their mouths make you think of love. When you ask them where they are from, they tilt their heads and say "Mobile" and you think you've been kissed. They say "Aiken" and you see a white butterfly glance off a fence with a torn wing. They say "Nagadoches" and you want to say "Yes, I will." You don't know what these towns are like, but you love what happens to the air when they open their lips and let the names ease out. (67)

Female speech, as Morrison renders it, is equivalent to what Cixous calls the "eternal essence," that feminine quality of bringing language down to earth and making it "playful." It also corresponds to Kristeva's definition of the semiotic in *Polylogue* as "a distinctive, non-expressive articulation. . . . We imagine it in infants' cries, vocalizing, and gestures; it functions in adult discourse as rhythm, prosody, word plays, the non-sense of sense, laughter" (14).

Mary Helen Washington maintains that there is a "generational continuity" among black women in which "one's mother serves as the female precursor who passes on the authority of authorship to her daughter and provides a model for the black woman's literary presence in this society" (147). Similarly, according to Kristeva, the "symbolic" as a form of communication is merely an acknowledgment of the language and the law of the father; it constitutes the repression of the "semiotic" which remains the province of the preoedipal phase, the world of the mother passed down to her daughters. According to Temma Berg as she interprets French theory in *Engendering the Word: Feminist Essays in Psychosexual Poetics*, "The fluidity of the preoedipal union with the mother offers the daughter an image of her body and of the language she needs to learn to use. Defined by woman's sexual difference, woman's language would be fluid, disorderly, sensual" (9). And, according to Berg and other theorists, and I think according to Morrison as well, the use of such language "will lead to the subversion of the closure of traditional Western metaphysics" (9).

In all her novels, Morrison implies the primacy of the maternal and the semiotic in the economy of language in order to achieve signification and a higher form of poetic (and also political) truth. As Kristeva writes in *Desire in Language*, "this relationship of the speaker to the mother is probably one of the most important factors producing interplay within the structure of meaning as well as a questioning process of subject and history" (137). Beyond the male "I" and outside of the metaphysics of binary opposition of Western humanism lies Kristeva's "she-truth" of the semiotic and, also, Morrison's mother-wit of the conjure woman, the expression of which is so central in her novels. Kristeva writes, in *Desire in Language*:

> No language can sing unless it confronts the Phallic Mother. For all that it must not leave her untouched, outside, opposite, against the law, the absolute esoteric code. Rather it must swallow her, eat her, dissolve her, set her up like a boundary of the process where "I" with "she"—"the other," "the mother"— becomes lost. Who is capable of this? "I alone am nourished by the great mother," writes Lao Tzu. (19)

As Cixous also says of the writer of feminine discourse, "There is always within her at least a little of that good mother's milk. She writes in white ink" (1986, 312).

What most wrenches the heart about Pecola in *The Bluest Eye* is not her poverty and her madness, but her motherlessness and her silence.[1] There is no adequate mother to teach her the feminine language, no preoedipal bonding to help her love herself and her body. As surrogate, she has only the "three merry gargoyles" (47), the "whores in whore's clothing" (48), to sing to her or to tell the stories that unmask the lie of the other story contained in the Dick and Jane reader, the unmusical and finally nonsensical words of which begin each chapter. The prostitutes and their stories cannot save Pecola, but they provide the only laughter in her life, and that laughter is yet another primal sound which transcends language, "like the sound of many rivers, freely, deeply, muddily, heading for the room of an open sea" (45).

Just as Pecola haunts the upstairs apartment of the three whores, seeking the laughter and the maternal space, so Milkman, living as he does in the oedipal nightmare of his family, seeks out the preoedipal arrangement of Pilate's family of women and also Pilate's mother-wit, the forbidden fruit of her knowledge, the orange she peels, the fruity wine she sells, and the perfect egg she offers. She wears a black dress and sits "wide-legged," suggestive of a birth position, and Milkman recognizes immediately that she transcends the law and the language of the father: "with the earring, the orange, and the angled black cloth, nothing—not the wisdom of his father nor the caution of the world—could keep him from her" (36). Her words are hypnotic, beyond language, and Milkman is charmed, bewitched, enthralled: "The piney-winey smell was narcotic, and so was the sun" (40). And Pilate teaches Milkman about language, that there are "five or six kinds of black. Some silky, some wooly. Some just empty" (40). As Pilate is the language-giver, she is also Milkman's spiritual mother, and on a literal level is responsible for his birth, having administered the aphrodisiac which united his parents and having made the voodoo doll which kept his father from killing him in the womb; she is also the primal mother, as Charles Scruggs notes, comparable to "the only other woman in history without a navel, Eve" (320).

The forbidden fruit Pilate gives to Milkman is a knowledge which is both more and less than that he seeks, his quest being information about his past and the past of his ancestors. She (and also the ageless Circe, another Eve figure and also a tale-telling woman) directs him to the maternal space of a cave in which he might discover gold, a bag of bones, an echo, or the ghost of his grandfather, but certainly the treasure of knowledge, even if the significance of that knowledge is lost on the unprepared boy. This cave, like the watery tunnel in *Sula* in which so many citizens of Medallion, lured by Shadrack's song, lose their lives, is an obvious womb symbol, but also more complex than that. For Morrison, the relationship with the mother is always ambiguous, revelatory yet destructive, even for women; but the male desire to return to the womb, to reenter the mother, is more often negatively associated with a surrender of consciousness or a death wish: "a big man can't be a baby all wrapped up inside his mama no more; he suffocate" (*Sula*, 62).

Death also is the dominant image in the first pages of *Tar Baby*, as the significantly named Son tries to birth himself from the sea, struggling from the vortex through "water, blood-tinted by a sun sliding into it like a fresh heart" and then darkness: "He knew he was in a part of the world that had never known and would never know twilight" (2). At the end of the novel, beaten by a world in which there is no place for him, abandoned by Jadine, Son returns to the mother, reenters the womb symbolized by the swamp that the Haitians have named "Sein de Vieilles. And witch's tit it was: a shriveled fogbound oval seeping with a thick black substance that even mosquitoes could not live near" (8), just as he has been directed by the conjure woman, Thérèse, who retains the archaic language and whose ancient breasts still give milk, images that link her also with the primal mother.[2]

What Milkman finds in the pit of the cave to which Pilate has directed him in *Song of Solomon* is even more negating and, to him, even more totally terrifying than the probable annihilation that Son runs so eagerly to meet. Milkman finds, not the bag of gold he has anticipated, nor the values of the father which such wealth represents, but that "There was nothing. Nothing at all. And before he knew it, he was hollering a long *awwww* sound into the pit" (255). This also is the birth cry, the primal scream that represents pain, that triggers bats, that greets the "too bright" light of the world.

The space of the mother is as equally ambiguous and problematic for a number of theorists as it is for Morrison; Kristeva, for one, although she celebrates both the biological condition and the metaphorical implications of motherhood, warns that women must challenge the "myth of the archaic mother." Woman, Kristeva writes in "Women's Time," "does not exist with a capital 'W', possessor of some mythical unity—a supreme power, on which is based the terror of power and terrorism as the desire for power. But what an unbelievable force for subversion in the modern world! And, at the same time, what playing with fire!" (205). Playing with fire, indeed, as Plum learns in *Sula* as he feels the benediction, the blessing of the kerosene on his skin, the love of the mother who strikes the match.

Existence in maternal space is less a problem for Morrison's female characters, most of the central figures living in the houses of their mothers and their grandmothers, comfortable with the female worlds and the matriarchal social structures these houses represent. Inevitably, the houses themselves exude exoticism, just as do the women who live in them. The "house of many rooms" (*Sula*, 26) in which Sula lives with Eva and Hannah is as whimsically constructed, with gratuitous stairways and doorways, as the lives of its inhabitants, and it is a testament to female power and autonomy in its refutation of male logic and practicality. Similarly, Pilate's house, which she shares with Reba and Hagar, is defined as female space; empty of furniture, on the edge of the black community and therefore of both the black and the dominant cultures, it is characterized by the pervasive presence of sunshine and the smell of pine trees. Baby Suggs's house in *Beloved*, where Sethe comes to live with her daughters, is inhospitable to males in general; Sethe's sons flee its confines on the first page of the novel, and it is not the baby ghost alone that at first prevents Paul D from entering and, finally, from being able to sleep or live at 124 Bluestone Road; for, as the first sentence of the novel makes clear, "124 was spiteful" (3).

As we shall also see in later chapters, this pattern of women living communally, which Morrison depicts with such frequency, is an arrangement that is not unusual given the historical and sociological realities of African American economic exigency. However, the persistence of the female triad as image in Morrison's fiction has also to do with an inquiry into the dangerous secrets of women's lives, their ways of knowing, and especially into their language and the wisdom and truth it expresses. The semiotic may be equated with the instinctual desire for the mother, the unconscious wish to enter the *chora* which is the maternal space,

that same space which Berg defines as "the space of the unconscious, the common language of the dream, the poetry we all
read/write" (13). According to Berg, the "woman's language" as
defined by French theorists is that which "enables us to reenter
Plato's cave, from which the 'good' male philosopher has expelled
us. The cave becomes the womb, the womb from which we seek
consciously to escape and to which we struggle unconsciously to
return" (9).

Ambiguities, as we have seen, are inherent in the image, and
in Morrison's novels the maternal space, even for women, is
fraught with danger as well as with desire. Sula's death, for example, is still a death, imbued though it is with the erotic potential of union with the mother. Curled into a fetal position, lying
in her grandmother's bed and in her grandmother's room, thumb
in her mouth, Sula reenters the womb of death:

> It would be here, only here, held by this blind window high
> above the elm tree, that she might draw her legs up to her chest,
> close her eyes, put her thumb in her mouth and float over and
> down the tunnels, just missing the dark walls, down, down un-
> til she met a rain scent and would know the water was near, and
> she would curl into its heavy softness and it would envelop her,
> carry her, and wash her tired flesh always. (128)

For the child, Denver, in *Beloved*, the womb space is at first
sweet and full of secrets. Just outside of her mother's house, a ring
of trees forms a narrow room, a cave of "emerald light": "In that
bower, closed off from the hurt of the hurt world, Denver's
imagination produced its own hunger and its own food, which
she badly needed because loneliness wore her out. *Wore her out*.
Veiled and protected by the live green walls, she felt ripe and clear,
and salvation was as easy as a wish" (28–29). Eventually Denver
leaves the female space of Sethe's house—her "salvation" lies after
all in a confrontation with a larger world—but not, however, until she has learned the mother tongue, drunk the mother's milk,
mixed though it literally is with blood. Such relationships are also
potentially damaging for the mother as well as for the daughter;
Sethe's other daughter's desire to reenter the womb almost kills
the mother. Although Sethe is a willing host, the community
women are correct in believing that "Sethe's dead daughter, the
one whose throat she cut, had come back to fix her. Sethe was

worn down, speckled, dying, spinning, changing shapes and generally bedeviled" (255). That which Beloved has sought in Sethe is the maternal space, the "loneliness that can be rocked. Arms crossed, knees drawn up; holding, holding on, the motion, unlike a ship's, smooths and contains the rocker. It's an inside kind—wrapped tight like skin" (274).

In *Beloved* it is the daughter who is the primary aggressor, but Denver is haunted also by a memory of maternal violence: "Her eye was on her mother, for a signal that the thing that was in her was out, and she would kill again" (240). Fear of maternal aggression, for both men and women, is as justifiable in Morrison's novels as it is in the work of a number of psychoanalysts, including Nancy J. Chodorow in *Feminism and Psychoanalytic Theory*: "cemented by maternal and infantile rage, motherhood becomes linked to destruction and death" (85). However, for both Morrison and Chodorow, female children are more likely than their brothers to survive, even benefit, from the encounter. While all children, Chodorow argues in *The Reproduction of Mothering*, are originally and essentially "matrisexual" (95), girls experience the preoedipal phase as less threatening than do boys: "Because of their mothering by women, girls come to experience themselves as less separate than boys, as having more permeable ego boundaries" (93). Chodorow quotes Freud's statement in "Female Sexuality": "One insight into this early pre-Oedipal phase in girls comes to us as a surprise, like the discovery in another field of the Minoan-Mycenaean civilization behind the civilization of Greece" (92).[3]

Morrison, too, renders this phase poetically, and in her novels it is not merely a phase but a condition of living, there being no interruption by the father in most instances, no violation of the feminine world of mothers and daughters by the oedipal law. And, always in Morrison, this preoedipal state encompasses space that is forbidden by the fathers; it is erotic, beyond masculine "law" and order, a wild zone. As we have seen, she depicts it in Eva's house in *Sula*, in Pilate's house in *Song of Solomon*, in Rosa's house in *Tar Baby*, but never so graphically as she does in *Beloved* when, after Paul D leaves Sethe's house, it becomes a veritable witch's nest, a semiotic jungle in which language itself defies convention and the laws of logic; voices merge and identities are indistinguishable:

> I am Beloved and she is mine. . . . I am not separate from
> her   there is no place where I stop   her face is my own and I
> want to be there in the place where her face is and to be look-
> ing at it too   a hot thing . . . she is the laugh   I am the
> laughter   I see her face which is mine . . . she knows I want to
> join   she chews and swallows me   I am gone   now I am her
> face   my own face has left me   I see me swim away   a hot
> thing   I see the bottoms of my feet   I am alone   I want to be
> the two of us   I want to join . . . a hot thing   now we can
> join   a hot thing. . . . (210–13)

It is not surprising that Stamp Paid cannot enter the house, for what he hears from outside is "a conflagration of hasty voices— loud, urgent, all speaking at once so he could not make out what they were talking about or to whom. The speech wasn't nonsen- sical, exactly, nor was it tongues. But something was wrong with the order of the words and he couldn't describe or cipher it to save his life" (172).[5] What Stamp Paid hears and what excludes him is the mother tongue, the feminine language, which, accord- ing to Cixous and Clément is "the resonance of fore-language. She lets the other language speak—the language of one thousand tongues which knows neither enclosure nor death" (317).

Later, Stamp Paid decides that what he has heard is the "mumbling of the black and angry dead," a natural response to white people, who, he says, believe that "under every dark skin was a jungle. Swift unnavigable waters, swinging screaming ba- boons, sleeping snakes, red gums ready for their sweet white blood. In a way, he thought, they were right. . . . But it wasn't the jungle blacks brought with them to this place from the other (livable) place. It was the jungle whitefolks planted in them. And it grew. It spread" (198). Stamp Paid is only partly right; it is not merely a black jungle he intuits, but a black *woman's* jungle, a linguistic wilderness, the mumbo-jumbo of the conjure world, "the thoughts of the women of 124, unspeakable thoughts, un- spoken" (199). When, finally, Denver understands that she must extricate herself from this preoedipal stew or starve to death, it is like stepping "off the edge of the world" (239).

Also in the case of the motherless Jadine/Jade in *Tar Baby*, guilt-ridden and haunted as she is by her visions of the African mothers and by her own departure from the values they represent, the dark womb is a source of hysteria. Sheer panic is her reaction to being sucked into quicksand in the same swamp on Isle des Chevaliers into which Son is later to run so eagerly; that pit of "moss-covered jelly" is no source of poetic truth for Jadine, but instead represents the possibility of a terrifying death, suffocation in "slime"; it is the locus of worms, snakes, and crocodiles (156). In Eloe, Florida, that island of African culture in America, and in Rosa's house, that image of maternal space, Jadine is similarly oppressed and terrified, suffocated in a tiny, womblike room where she wakes to find "the blackest nothing she had ever seen. . . . It's not possible, she thought, for anything to be this black. . . . She might as well have been in a cave, a grave, the dark womb of the earth, suffocating with the sound of plant life moving, but deprived of its sight" (216–17). Morrison indicates, however, that Jadine's hysteria is a result of her own inability to choose an identity, whether black or white, and her aversion to maternal space is both cause and symptom for her fragmentation. Jadine never sings, and her conversation is "educated," too white, too superficial, too removed from the mother tongue. As Ondine tells her: "Jadine, a girl has got to be a daughter first. She have to learn that. And if she never learns how to be a daughter, she can't never learn how to be a woman" (242).

Not focused upon but powerfully present in its intimations, one of the significant silences and potent gaps in *Sula*, is Helene Wright's rejection of the preoedipal bond, her refusal to recognize in language her relationship with the Creole-speaking prostitute in the canary-yellow dress who is her mother. Nel is enchanted by the dress, the gardenia smell, and the exotic language, but Helene rejects them all: "I don't talk Creole. . . . And neither do you" (23). Perhaps Nel's cry in the last lines of the novel, a primal scream beyond and above language, a cry Jadine has forgotten but that Beloved well remembers, is a reinstatement of the semiotic from which her own mother has separated her as well as herself: "It was a fine cry—loud and long—but it had no bottom and it had no top, just circles and circles of sorrow" (149).

Sula's own similar "howl" experienced at the moment of orgasm is also a primal scream with its origins in the mother-tongue. According to Mae Gwendolyn Henderson: "It is through the howl of orgasm that Sula discovers a prediscursive center of experience that positions her at the vantage point outside of the dominant discursive order. The howl is a form of speaking in tongues and a linguistic disruption that serves as the precondition for Sula's entry into language" (33). Henderson further theorizes that Sula's cry constitutes a "womblike matrix" in which "soundlessness can be transformed into utterance, unity into diversity, formlessness into form, chaos into art, silence into tongues, and glossolalia into heteroglossia" (35–36). Sula's howl is like Pilate's toward the end of *Song of Solomon*, a statement of the loss of Hagar but also of universal loss, a cry for "Mercy!" that resonates from the unconscious, from the "jungle" part of Pilate's mind:

> Suddenly, like an elephant who has just found his anger and lifts his trunk over the heads of the little men who want his teeth or his hide or his flesh or his amazing strength, Pilate trumpeted for the sky itself to hear, "And she was *loved!*"
> It startled one of the sympathetic winos in the vestibule and he dropped his bottle, spurting emerald glass and jungle-red wine everywhere. (323)

The primal cry, the loss of intelligible language, often effected by the return, willing or unwilling, to maternal space, is as problematic and as fraught with danger and with the potential for hysteria for most French theorists as it is for Morrison. Alice Jardine explains Kristeva's thoughts as follows:

> For Kristeva, the moments when women deny culture, reject theory, exalt the body, and so forth are moments when they risk crossing over the cultural borderline into hysteria. While recognizing hysteria as potentially liberating and as one of the major forms of contestation throughout our history, she also relentlessly emphasizes its very real limits: the fantasy of the phallic, all-powerful mother through which women reconnect with the very Law they had set out to fight. . . . (1980, 11)

Yet, even for Kristeva, the transformation of the symbolic order is necessary, and she repeatedly argues that women must let what she calls the "spasmodic force of the unconscious," experienced through the link with the preoedipal mother figure, prevail and disrupt their language in order that they may emerge sexually and politically transformed.

Hysteria itself can function as an agent of such transformation. For Cixous in "Castration or Decapitation?" "The hysteric is a divine spirit that is always at the edge, the turning point, of making" (47). If hysteria results in silence, that, too, is a form of discourse: "Silence: silence is the mark of hysteria. The great hysterics have lost speech, they are aphonic, and at times have lost more than speech: they are pushed to the point of choking, nothing gets through. They are decapitated, their tongues are cut off and what talks isn't heard because it's the body that talks, and man doesn't hear the body" (49).

All of Morrison's works are about silence as well as about language, whether that silence is metaphysical or physically enforced by circumstance.[6] All African Americans, like a great many immigrants to America, write and speak in a language they do not own as theirs. Women too, perhaps, speak generally in a language not their own but which belongs to a male culture. Historically, the dominant culture has enforced black and female silence through illiteracy as well as through hysteria, through the metaphoric and actual insertion of the bit in the mouth which inevitably results in "the wildness that shot up into the eye the moment the lips were yanked back" (*Beloved*, 71). The point of Morrison's novels, in fact, is to give a voice to the voiceless, to speak the unspeakable on the part of the speechless, to tell just "how offended the tongue is, held down by iron" (*Beloved*, 71).

Pecola Breedlove in *The Bluest Eye*, for example, does not tell her own story or even speak much beyond monosyllables. Among the poignant scenes in the novel is that in which Pecola confronts the white owner of the candy store and can only point or nod in the direction of the Mary Janes she covets. "Christ. Kantcha talk?" he demands, and, in fact, Pecola cannot talk; her almost perpetual silence prefigures the condition of hysteria in which she ends, "picking and plucking her way between the tire rims and the sunflowers, between Coke bottles and milkweed, among all the waste and beauty of the world—which is what she herself was" (159). Pecola's silence, broken only in her insane discourse with an imaginary friend who reassures her that in fact her eyes are blue and therefore beautiful, surely is intended to represent the muted condition of all women as well as the powerlessness of children in the face of cruelty and neglect, and to indict a dominant culture that values speech over silence and presence over absence.

Because Pecola is so effectively muted, the novel is narrated by Claudia, who recognizes her complicity and that of the rest of the community of Lorain, Ohio, in contributing to Pecola's hysteria through its almost malicious refusal to provide either love or charity. Even though Claudia's narration is most often in present tense and she presents herself as a child, the reader accepts that the teller is working through memory, is now grown and capable of the poetic and sophisticated imagery she commands. Yet, still, Claudia doubts her own authenticity; occasionally the present tense is interrupted by interjections: "But was it really like that? As painful as I remember?" (14). In her summation at the novel's end, Claudia wonders whether she has not "rearranged lies and called it truth, seeing in the new pattern of an old idea the Revelation and the Word" (159). Almost as if by way of correction, Pecola's story is also told by implication in the first-person narration of her mother, as well as by a disembodied and nameless omniscience, whose word we can never doubt. This narrator, like Claudia, and like Morrison herself in all her fictions, operates within a "new pattern of an old idea," a reinscription of the Word itself which is also, paradoxically, a silence.

Henry Louis Gates, Jr., writes that much of black literature is distinguished by the stylistic use of the trope that is not "the presence of voice at all, but its absence. To speak of a silent voice is to speak in an oxymoron" (1988, 167). As Gates theorizes, blackness, like silence, signifies absence as well as racial identity within the symbolic order. In *The Bluest Eye*, Pecola cannot be heard, but she also cannot be *seen* by the candy seller: "He does not see her, because for him there is nothing to see. . . . And it is the blackness that accounts for, that creates, the vacuum edged with distaste in white eyes" (42). What is *not* seen in this novel, so imbued with the significance of vision, is as important as what *is* seen. Because of her self-perceived ugliness and because others see her as ugly as well, Pecola wishes, even prays, to become an absence, to disappear: "'Please, God,' she whispered into the palm of her hand. 'Please make me disappear'" (39).

That which has disappeared, is absent, silent, or invisible—what Morrison calls "the void that is Pecola's 'unbeing'" (1990, 220)—pervades the novel: Pauline Breedlove's unhappy life is determined by the absence of a tooth rather than by the presence of the crippled foot she blames for her misfortunes; a lack of blue eyes and her inability to conform to white standards of beauty as represented by the chimera of an absent Shirley Temple contribute to Pecola's loss of sanity; rather than a cry or a word, there is silence, only the "hollow suck of air in the back of her throat" (128) as Pecola is raped by her father; the universal deprivation of the Dick-and-Jane-reader image of the pretty green and white house with the red door is the cause rather than the effect of historical suffering; the novel opens and closes with references to the marigolds that do *not* grow in 1941.

Sula, too, is a novel about absence as well as about presence, and, like *The Bluest Eye*, it inverts a system of thought and values that can entertain only the viability of presence. The very setting of the story, the neighborhood of the Bottom in Medallion, Ohio, no longer exists at the time of the telling, nor do its "nightshade and blackberry patches," nor the beech trees, nor Irene's Palace of Cosmetology, all having been replaced by the Medallion City Golf Course. More than nostalgia has been established by their absence, for now the Bottom is part of myth and memory, and, as such, it becomes a kind of center, a world navel, a cosmic omphalos, a "Medallion" in fact. The "nigger joke" told on the first page of the novel is really on the white man who thought he lied when he said that this land was "the bottom of heaven" (5).

Sula, the "central" character, is also defined by absence, having "no center, no speck around which to grow" (103). She is literally absent for ten years of the novel's action, her whereabouts only vaguely accounted for, and she dies three-quarters of the way through. Among the significant moments of her life is not the killing, however accidental, of Chicken Little, but her recognition of the "closed place in the water" where he has disappeared, the "something newly missing" (52). Even orgasm for Sula is defined by silence and by absence—a "howl" that is paradoxically "soundlessness," a transcendence of the "word"—and by a recognition of something missing or lost: "she leaped from the edge into soundlessness and went down howling, howling in a stinging awareness of the endings of things: an eye of sorrow in the midst of all that hurricane of rage and joy. There, in the center of that silence was not eternity but the death of time and a loneliness so profound the word itself had no meaning" (106).

For both Sula and Nel, life and its choices are defined more by what they are *not* than by what they are; being "neither white nor male, and that all freedom and triumph was forbidden to them, they had set about creating something else to be" (44). Shadrack, too, is defined by negation: "with no past, no language, no tribe, no source, no address book, no comb, no pencil, no clock, no pocket handkerchief, no rug, no bed, no can opener, no faded postcard, no soap, no key, no tobacco pouch, no soiled underwear and nothing nothing nothing to do" (10). Relationships, like that between Sula and Nel, or between Nel and Jude, are a matter of filling spaces, the "space in front of me, behind me, in my head" (124). Much more significant for Sula than Ajax's presence is his absence, which "was everywhere, stinging everything, giving the furnishings primary colors, sharp outlines to the corners of rooms and gold light to the dust collecting on table tops" (116). Where does Ajax go when he leaves Sula, or Jude when he leaves Nel, and where was Eva when she lost her leg? Morrison explains in "The Afro-American Presence in American Literature" that "invisible things are not necessarily 'not-there'; that a void may be empty, but is not a vacuum. In addition, certain absences are so stressed, so ornate, so planned, they call attention to themselves; arrest us with intentionality and purpose . . ." (1990, 210).

Most obviously in *Sula*, there is the absence of Eva Peace's leg, the other rendered more glamorous by "the long fall of space below her left thigh" (27); it is this missing limb which may well be responsible for Eva's attainment of money and therefore of power, but it is also her refusal to *tell* how and why she lost the leg that accounts for her status in the community and her mythic presence in the novel. Marianne Hirsch, in *The Mother/Daughter Plot*, argues convincingly that communication between mothers and daughters is always characterized by silence and based on "the unspeakable," and in *Sula*, "Eva's missing leg is the mark of maternal discourse in the novel and the key to its (thematized) ambivalence toward it" (179). According to Houston A. Baker, Jr., Eva's missing leg is itself a challenge to patriarchy and to capitalism, an "utterance of the *Non Servium*," a conversion of her body "into a dismembered instrument of defiance—and finance" (91).

In *Song of Solomon*, places as well as people are defined by what they are not: "Not Doctor Street" and "No Mercy Hospital" are both terms of passive resistance, defiance hurled in the teeth of white officialdom. But the most important absence in this novel is the smooth, bare space on the stomach of Pilate Dead, that place where a navel should have been. So dominant is this absence in her life that it dictates her position on the margins of her community, while it also defines her mythological status as a woman who gave birth to herself, who "began at zero" (149). Like the white spaces in Chinese paintings that define their shapes and designs, absence defines the form of this novel as well as Pilate's significance at its center. The "nothing" that Milkman Dead finds at the center of the cave, the center of maternal space to which Pilate directs him, is, in reality, everything, the perfect circle, the mystical zero without which numbers, and indeed all logic and knowing, are impossible.[7]

Clearly, the significant silences and the stunning absences throughout Morrison's texts become profoundly political as well as stylistically crucial. Morrison describes her own work as containing "holes and spaces so the reader can come into it" (Tate 1989, 125), testament to her rejection of theories that privilege the author over the reader. Morrison disdains such hierarchies in which the reader as participant in the text is ignored: "My writing expects, demands participatory reading, and I think that is what literature is supposed to do. It's not just about telling the story; it's about involving the reader . . . we (you, the reader, and I, the author) come together to make this book, to feel this experience" (Tate 1989, 125). But Morrison also indicates in each of her novels that images of the zero, the absence, the silence that is both chosen and enforced, are ideologically and politically revelatory. The history of slavery itself, Morrison writes in *Beloved*, is "not a story to pass on" but, rather, is something that is "unspeakable," unconscionable, unbearable. Among the heinous crimes of slavery was its silencing of its victims; how perversely ironic it is that "Schoolteacher" does not come to Sweet Home to teach literacy, but to take notes, to do scholarship on the measurement of black craniums. Ironic, too, is the fact that Schoolteacher's notes are taken in ink that Sethe, herself quite possibly functionally illiterate, has manufactured. Paul D cannot read the newspaper account of Sethe's crime, and, even in freedom, Denver must lurk outside and beneath the window of the reading teacher's house.

Morrison's characters are most frequently politically muted in spite of the lyrical language of the mother she always provides for them. They themselves do not articulate, or perhaps realize, the political ramifications of certain of their actions, but Morrison repeatedly translates the body itself into political "speech." Eva's act of self-mutilation in *Sula*, for example, is motivated by a will to survive, but the effect is also a statement indicting poverty and the conditions of life for black women. As Eva endures the amputation of her leg, so Sula slices off the tip of her own finger, ostensibly to protect herself and Nel from abusive white boys, but also effectively to issue a warning, to use her body as a language. And Sethe in *Beloved* trades ten minutes of sex for a single inscription, "the one word that mattered" (5), on her daughter's tombstone, thus almost literally translating her body into the written word. Sethe's motivation for murdering her child is, obviously, a desperate attempt to protect that child from what she considers a fate far worse than death; but, as we shall see in Chapter 3, Morrison renders this act also as the ultimate statement, the most significant transcendence of the word, an act of the body that, like slavery itself, is truly "unspeakable."

Silence exists also in the text of *Beloved* itself, as, according to Wilfred D. Samuels and Clenora Hudson-Weems, was the case in the original slave narratives, characterized by "not what history has recorded . . . but what it has omitted" (96). Samuels and Hudson-Weems quote Morrison as saying of slave narratives: "somebody forgot to tell somebody something. . . . My job becomes how to rip that veil" (97). But Morrison's own "veils," indicative of the kind of pain the writing of *Beloved* entailed, remain implicit in the text, which itself is a revision, an inversion, and, finally, a subversion of traditional value systems that privilege presence over absence and speech over silence.[8] The central paradox, however, is that the silence of women echoes with reverberation, speaks louder than words: "What a roaring," writes Morrison in *Beloved* (181).

Reverberation is that quality which characterizes all of Morrison's fictions—what is left unsaid is equally as important as what is stated and specified; what is felt is as significant as what is experienced; what is dreamed is as valid as what transpires in the world of "fact." And none of these conditions of being is rendered as opposite; there are no polarities between logic and mysticism, between real and fantastic. Rather, experience for Morrison's characters is the acceptance of a continuum, a recognition that the mind is not separate from the body or the real separate from that which the imagination can conceive. She writes from the maternal space, which is consciousness but also the unconscious, the dream world; but those dreams have substance, teeth, and they are part

of a world conception in which terms like "fact" seem superflu-
ous. In Chapter 3, we shall see that "magic realism" is not, for
Morrison, an oxymoron. In an interview with Grace Epstein,
Morrison talks about the significance of dreams, their practical
value for winning at the numbers game when she was a child in
Lorain, Ohio, and about how their validity was unquestioned,
particularly by her mother, who "thought" rather than "dreamed"
her sleeping experiences:

> It was like the second life she was living, so that dreamscape,
> then, becomes accessible, a separate part, and it's functional in
> some respects. As a child the problem is trying to establish what
> is real and what is not real. Since my dreams were real in the
> sense they were about *reality*, some dream life could spill over
> into the regular life; that's where the enchantment came from. (5)

All of Morrison's fictions partake of a dreamscape, contain a
quality that is surreal at times, largely because of this refusal to
mark dreams as distinct or separate from "reality."[9] There are
some dreams—in *Sula*, for example, in which Hannah dreams her
own death by fire as "a wedding in a red bridal gown" (63)—
that serve as predictions; but these are exceptions. Narrative itself
is dreamlike: diffused, fluid, always erotic. In one sense, Morrison's novels serve as the reader's own dreams, where that which
is repressed, contained, becomes consciously expressed. Irigaray
writes about the dream quality of the feminine text as a reflection
of the feminine sensibility: "women diffuse themselves according
to modalities scarcely compatible with the framework of the rul-
ing symbolics. Which doesn't happen without causing some tur-
bulence, we might even say some whirlwinds, that ought to be
reconfined within solid walls of principle, to keep them from
spreading to infinity" (1985, 106).

Morrison's language does, in essence, spread to "infinity,"
and the prevalent image of flight in all her novels is more than a
symbol for freedom or for ambition. Airplanes, birds, anything
that flies, become signifiers for the flight of language itself, for the
movement beyond linguistic boundaries, for the untraditional
style and structure of Morrison's work. Cixous writes, "Flying is
a woman's gesture—flying in language and making it fly" (1986,
316). While Morrison's language soars in *The Bluest Eye*, little
Pecola, without a language, can only aspire to a grotesque imita-

tion of flight: "Elbows bent, hands on shoulders, she flailed her arms like a bird in an eternal, grotesquely futile effort to fly. Beating the air, a winged but grounded bird, intent on the blue void it could not reach—could not even see—but which filled the valleys of the mind" (158).

Morrison's male characters, too, imagine themselves in flight and are almost all in love with airplanes. Ajax in *Sula* loves his mother, and "after her—airplanes. There was nothing in between" (109). In the tradition of black literature since Richard Wright's *Native Son*, however, the privilege of flight, at least in airplanes, is mostly reserved for white boys. Black males, in Morrison, fly only metaphorically, and then only with the assistance and the inspiration of black women. According to Baker, in his aptly titled "When Lindbergh Sleeps with Bessie Smith," "flight is a function of black woman's conjure and not black male industrial initiative" (105). The only male character in *Sula* permitted flight pays with his life; Sula picks up Chicken Little and swings him out over the water, letting go (accidentally) at that precise moment when his joy is greatest: "His knickers ballooned and shrieks of frightened joy startled the birds and the fat grasshoppers. When he slipped from her hands and sailed away out over the water they could still hear his bubbly laughter" (52). Sula alone in this novel is capable of seeing "the slant of life that made it possible to stretch it to its limits"; she only has the ability to "free fall," to complete that action "that required—demanded—invention: a thing to do with the wings, a way of holding the legs and most of all a full surrender to the downward flight," and this act only can allow the flyer to "taste the tongue or stay alive" (103–4).

Song of Solomon opens with the image of attempted flight, as Robert Smith, ironically an agent of the North Carolina Mutual Life Insurance company, promises to "take off from Mercy and fly away on my own wings" (3). Pilate (Pilot?) does not save him (as the reader always hopes she might and believes she could), but she sings him to his death: "O Sugarman done fly / O Sugarman done gone," and he, at least, "had seen the rose petals, heard the music" (9). And Milkman Dead, born the next day in Mercy Hospital, the first "colored" baby ever to claim that distinction, must, Morrison says, have been marked by Mr. Smith's blue silk wings, for "when the little boy discovered, at four, the same thing Mr. Smith had learned earlier—that only birds and airplanes could fly—he lost all interest in himself" (9).

Years later, Milkman and his friend, Guitar, are amazed by the mysterious, even mystical appearance of a peacock over the building of the used car lot where they stand. As the bird descends, Milkman mistakes it for a female, but Guitar corrects him: "He. That's a he. The male is the only one got that tail full of jewelry. Son of a bitch." Milkman, in all his innocent conviction of male superiority, asks why the peacock can fly no better than a chicken, and Guitar, who wants to catch and eat the bird, answers, "Too much tail. All that jewelry weighs it down. Like vanity. Can't nobody fly with all that shit. Wanna fly, you got to give up the shit that weighs you down" (179–80).

Morrison permits Milkman at least one experience of actual flight, if only on a plane, but even then "the wings of all those other people's nightmares flapped in his face and constrained him" (222). Mostly, Milkman's flight fantasies are in the form of dreams, and they evoke womb images more than an idea of freedom:

> It was a warm dreamy sleep all about flying, about sailing high over the earth. But not with arms stretched out like airplane wings, nor shot forward like Superman in a horizontal dive, but floating, cruising, in the relaxed position of a man lying on a couch reading a newspaper. Part of his flight was over the dark sea, but it didn't frighten him because he knew he could not fall. He was alone in the sky, but somebody was applauding him, watching him and applauding. (302)

In order to truly fly, however, Milkman must give up his male vanities, "the shit that weighs [him] down"; it is necessary to placate the violated female essence of his universe, atone for his mistreatment of Hagar, apologize for his failure to recognize the humanity of his sisters and his mother, exorcise the influence of his father, and embrace the teachings of Pilate, who is surely the one applauding and watching in Milkman's dream.

Whether or not Milkman fulfills these requirements, becomes a better human being, and actually flies as a reward on the last page of the novel is a subject for a great deal of critical controversy. According to Cynthia A. Davis, Milkman truly flies, and he represents the traditional mythic hero:

> Milkman's life follows the pattern of the classic hero, from miraculous birth (he is the first black baby born in Mercy Hospital, on a day marked by song, rose petals in the snow, and human "flight") through quest-journey to final reunion with his double. And Milkman largely resolves the conflict between freedom and connection . . . he finds that his quest is his culture's; he can only discover what he is by discovering what his family is. By undertaking the quest, he combines subjective freedom with objective fact and defines himself in both spheres. . . . Only in the recognition of his condition can he act in it, only in commitment is he free. (333–34)

But even among classical heroes, there is the possibility of failure in flight, and Icarus always looms as example. At the opposite extreme of interpretation from Davis's analysis is that by Gerry Brenner, who argues that Morrison's treatment of Milkman is purely ironic, and that her attitude toward his search for his "gene pool" is one of disdain. Even the image of flight, in Brenner's analysis, is pejorative, representing "man's prerogative—to escape domestication, to fly from responsibility, in the name of self-fulfillment or self-discovery or self-indulgence . . . he flies, indeed, from the burdens of doing something meaningful in life, preferring the sumptuous illusion that he will ride the air" (119). Morrison herself indicates that her rendering of myth in this novel is indeed ironic: "Sotto (but not completely) is my own giggle (in Afro-American terms) of the proto-myth of the journey to manhood. Whenever characters are cloaked in Western fable, they are in deep trouble; but the African myth is also contaminated" (1990, 226). Also evidence that Morrison's rendering of Milkman's character is ironic can be found in her own statement: "I chose the man to make that journey because I thought he had more to learn than a woman would have" (McKay, 428).

Certainly women suffer as a result of the male desire for flight. Milkman's ancestor, Solomon/Shalimar, was one of numerous slaves from Africa who could fly; according to the story Milkman is told, Solomon launched himself into the air from a cotton field one day, leaving behind his wife and twenty-one children. The cry of the abandoned woman, another primal scream from the jungle of female discourse, still echoes throughout the land in Ryna's Gulch, a testament to the irresponsibility of men and the proclivity of women to love them. Milkman, too, has abandoned every woman in his life, including the convenient Sweet, who warms the bed and bathes his body in the last sections of the novel. Pilate alone is the woman/mother who commands Milkman's respect and his love, for "Without ever leaving the ground, she could fly" (340).

Whether or not Milkman "rides the air" in the last lines, or whether he reenacts the suicide of Robert Smith on page one, jumping into space and delivering himself into "the killing arms of his brother," is, finally, ambiguous. Were Morrison to resolve this novel so neatly with Milkman's complete regeneration and reward, the reader's expectations about her recurrent and pervasive use of paradox, her refusal in every novel to adopt novelistic conventions about closure and resolution, would be disappointed. Significant to Morrison's great strength as a writer is the fact that her style is imbued with contradiction and saturated with breaches of narrative continuity. And, according to Irigaray, a feminine style of writing, is "always *fluid*," always "resists and explodes every firmly established form, figure, idea, or concept" to the point that "linear reading is no longer possible" (1985, 79–80).

As we shall also see in a later chapter on Morrison's rendering of history, concepts like linearity, progress, chronology, even development, are not primarily valuable in an analysis of her works, nor do they form a pattern for the structure of her novels. Morrison's structures are almost always circular, diffuse, organized by a radical standard of that which constitutes order. (This study, too, is deliberately arranged thematically rather than chronologically, in deference to Morrison's style and in an attempt to discount linearity as a value.) It would be worse than useless, for example, to talk about "plot development" in Morrison's novels; there *is* plot, certainly, but its revelation *culminates* or evolves through a process of compilation of multiple points of view, varieties of interpretation of events (and some of these contradictory), through repetition and reiteration. As there is no "climax," in the usual sense, so also there is no resolution, no series of events that can conveniently be labeled "beginning, middle, end." Cixous characterizes feminine writing in the following way: "A feminine textual body is recognized by the fact that it is always endless, without ending: there's no closure, it doesn't stop. . . . A feminine text starts on all sides, all at once, starts twenty times, thirty times, over" (1981, 53).

All of Morrison's novels embody a principle that defies closure: *The Bluest Eye* reveals in the second sentence that "Pecola was having her father's baby," and the rest of the text is an afterthought: "There is really nothing more to say—except why. But since why is difficult to handle, one must take refuge in how" (9). The "how," then, is explained from every perspective, including a historical one in which Pecola does not even participate as subject. Morrison explains her choice for the structure of this novel:

> I tell you at the beginning of *The Bluest Eye* on the very first page what happened, but now I want you to go with me and look at this, so when you get to the scene where the father rapes the daughter, which is as awful a thing, I suppose, as can be imagined, by the time you get there it's almost irrelevant because I want you to *look* at him and see his love for his daughter and his powerlessness to help her pain. By that time his embrace, the rape, is all the gift he has left. (Tate 1989, 125)

Morrison has also explained her intention of subverting the literary tradition of male rape fantasies through a use of feminine language: "It is interesting to me that where I thought I would have the most difficulty subverting the language to a feminine mode, I had the least: connecting Cholly's 'rape' by the white men to his own of his daughter. This most masculine act of aggression becomes feminized in my language, 'passive,' and, I think, more accurately repellent when deprived of the male 'glamor of shame' rape is (or once was) routinely given" (1990, 220).

Perspective and narrative responsibility in *Sula* are similarly "feminized" by being fragmented and multiple; the novel begins with a story from Shadrack's perspective, which has little, immediately, to do with Sula; Nel, and even Nel's mother, are also centers of consciousness at times only marginally concerned with Sula. Each event in the novel is similarly fragmented, related impressionistically, and thus this novel, like all of Morrison's works, subverts concepts of textual unity and defies totalized interpretation.

Tar Baby, too, has multiple centers, as well as multiple central characters whose histories are gradually revealed in fragments by a variety of sources. Secrets and silences and the failure of love comprise the province of each set of couples in the novel; Son and Jadine share the focus with Sydney and Ondine, Margaret and Valerian, and even with Thérèse and Gideon, all of whom lose identity in Morrison's concern for the central dyad, white and black, and even this opposition is blurred, merged, rendered less valid. Setting, too, in this novel is amorphous; whether the reader is in Isle des Chevaliers, Eloe, Florida, or in New York City ("if ever there was a black woman's town, New York was it" [191]), she is always in a world of myth, a place that is metaphorically "the end of the world" (7).

The same blurring of boundaries is true of *Beloved*, in which the personal history of Sethe and her daughters is revealed ever so gradually, fragmented into symbols, and, finally, becomes one with the history of all African Americans. Everyone tells or sings the story of slavery and the escape into a freedom that is also, paradoxically, still a form of slavery. And, each tale, each aspect of the monomyth, is retold, elaborated upon, rendered in circles and silences by every character in the novel; Sethe's recounting of her story to Paul D is accompanied by a physical act of making circles and is emblematic of all tale-telling in the novel: "At first he thought it was her spinning. Circling him the way she was circling the subject. Round and round, never changing direction, which might have helped his head . . . listening to her was like having a child whisper into your ear so close you could feel its lips form the words you couldn't make out because they were too close" (161). But the largest circle and the deepest secrets are those told us by that same enigmatic, pervasive omniscience which is Morrison herself.

Despite the ambiguity and the lack of resolution at the conclusion, *Song of Solomon* is, in form, more conventional than Morrison's other novels, styled as it is after the traditional bildungsroman and stressing as it does the education of a young man. Morrison has described her intentions with regard to the structure of her novels in the following way:

> The first two books were beginnings. I start with the childhood
> of a person in all the books; but in the first two, the movement,
> the rhythm, is circular, although the circles are broken. If you

go back to the beginnings, you get pushed along toward the end. This is particularly so with *The Bluest Eye*. *Sula* is more spiral than circular. *Song of Solomon* is different. I was trying to push this novel outward; its movement is neither circular nor spiral. The image in my mind for it is that of a train picking up speed; and that image informs the language; whereas with *The Bluest Eye* and *Sula*, the rhythm is very different. (Tate 1989, 124)

It is quite likely that Morrison's use of traditional novel structure in *Song of Solomon* is a deliberate subversion of the form itself, just as she has indicated that the style of the opening pages is a mock journalistic style (1990, 224). If, as was discussed earlier, Morrison's treatment of Milkman as a character is at least partially ironic, then there is also the possibility that her "imitation" of the bildungsroman, itself a gendered form, is parodic, carnivalesque, yet another indication of Milkman's privileged status within the realm of the symbolic, even though his quest, ultimately, is to escape what is not, after all, a privilege but a limitation.

Morrison's ironies, however, are always gentle, meant to heal rather than to wound, to correct rather than to punish. Her humor, like her use of language in general and like her departures from stylistic tradition, is nonetheless subversive, often sexually implicit (as we shall see in Chapter 4), certainly gendered. She takes her novelistic pleasure and provides the same for her readers, for her language is always a celebration of the laugh of the Medusa, even when her subjects are so serious, so tragic and intense, that they turn us to stone.

2

Hagar's Mirror: Self and Identity

One day Pilate sat down on Hagar's bed and held a compact before her granddaughter's face. It was trimmed in a goldlike metal and had a pink plastic lid.

"Look, baby. See here?" Pilate turned it all around to show it off and pressed in the catch. The lid sprang open and Hagar saw a tiny part of her face reflected in the mirror. She took the compact then and stared into the mirror for a long while.

"No wonder," she said at last. "Look at that. No wonder. No wonder."

— *Song of Solomon*

Mirrors are dangerous objects in Morrison's fictions. What destroys Hagar is not merely Pilate's oppressive love (her gift of the mirror being evidence of this) nor Milkman's failure to love, but the vision of herself as *self* that the mirror reflects. The mirror lies in telling her that she is not beautiful, for mirrors represent only white standards of beauty;[1] but the greater lie is that illusion of unified selfhood which mirrors also perpetrate, for the "self" in Morrison's fiction, like her use of language discussed in the preceding chapter, is always multiple, contradictory, and ambiguous—if, in fact, a self can be said to exist at all.

An interesting parallel to Hagar's mirror-death exists early in the same novel, at the point at which Milkman gazes at his own face in the mirror with at least mild approval of the "firm jaw line, splendid teeth" but largely unaware of what the narrator knows, that the image "lacked coherence, a coming together of the features into a total self" (69–70). According to Cixous and Clé-

35

ment in *The Newly Born Woman*, when a man looks into a mirror, he "identifies and constitutes himself with the mirror. It reflects his image to him, *fixes* it as a subject and subjects it to the law, to the symbolic order, to language, and does it in a way that is both inalienable and alienating" (137). Milkman's "self"-analysis is juxtaposed, significantly, to the entrance of his father, who surely represents for Morrison an exaggerated and clearly parodic version of patriarchal inscriptions, including those of identity and selfhood, most particularly the fiction that "You have to be a whole man. And if you want to be a whole man, you have to deal with the whole truth" (70).

Clearly, there are no "whole truths" or "whole" men and women in Morrison's novels, at least not in any traditional fictional sense. Just as she challenges the dominant cultural view of language and signification (as was discussed in the preceding chapter), so Morrison also subverts traditional Western notions of identity and wholeness. Patricia Waugh, in *Feminine Fictions: Revisiting the Postmodern*, is not alone in her observation that the death of the self is characteristic of all postmodern fictions, which thus act to undermine traditional philosophies by contradicting "the dualistic, objective posturing of western rationality" (22). More central to the present concern is Waugh's argument that "for those marginalized by the dominant culture, a sense of identity as constructed through impersonal and social relations of power (rather than a sense of identity as the reflection of an inner 'essence') has been a major aspect of their self-concept long before post-structuralists and postmodernists began to assemble their cultural manifestos" (3). If this is true particularly for women, as Waugh maintains, how much more radical might be the deconstruction of the self as a concept in fiction by those doubly marginalized by race as well as gender?

French theorists are among those who in recent years have radically undermined notions of the unitary self, notions they attribute directly to Western humanism, which they see as totally and unmitigatedly male in origin as well as in values. Irigaray, for example, condemns what she and many others term phallocentric literature as the "endless litigation over identity with oneself" (118). She defines feminine language by contrast as inherently multiple, based on the complex biology of women:

in that "syntax" there would no longer be either subject or object, "oneness" would no longer be privileged, there would no longer be proper meanings, proper names, "proper" attributes. . . . Instead, that "syntax" would involve nearness, proximity, but in such an extreme form that it would preclude any distinction of identities, any establishment of ownership, thus any form of appropriation. (134)

Alice Jardine, whose theoretical focus is an interpretation of French feminisms, characterizes their works as a "whirlpool of decentering" in which "The notion of the 'Self'—so intrinsic to Anglo-American thought, becomes absurd. It is not something called the 'Self' which speaks, but language, the unconscious, the 'textuality of the text'" (1986, 563). Toril Moi also analyzes French resistance to concepts of selfhood in terms of Lacan and Derrida, and writes:

As Luce Irigaray or Hélène Cixous would argue, this integrated self is in fact a phallic self, constructed on the model of the self-contained, powerful phallus. Gloriously autonomous, it banishes from itself all conflict, contradiction and ambiguity. In this humanist ideology the self is the *sole author* of history and of the literary text: the humanist creator is potent, phallic and male—God in relation to his world, the author in relation to his text. History or the text become nothing but "expression" of this unique individual: all art becomes autobiography, a mere window on to the self and the world, with no reality of its own. (1985, 8)

As she has made clear in a number of interviews, Morrison does not write autobiography.[2] As the author has no self that is manifested in her fiction, so also Morrison's narrators are most often unidentifiable, anonymous, vehicles to transmit information and convey emotion rather than to provide moral interpretations or represent a personality.[3] Often these narrators disappear completely as one character or another steps forward to tell the story from a different point of view. But even these speaking characters reflect multiple and fragmented selves, which are sometimes undefined, inevitably amorphous, always merging with the identity of a community as a whole or with the very concept of blackness. Henry Louis Gates, Jr., has commented on the irony of African

American writers attempting "to posit a 'black self' in the very
Western languages in which blackness itself is a figure of absence,
a negation" (1984, 7).

For example, in *Sula*, that point at which Nel looks into the
mirror and discovers her "me-ness" is almost as fraught with pre-
monition of disaster as when Hagar peers into the pink and gold
compact in *Song of Solomon*. For Nel, the mirror reflects, not a
concept called Nel, but something other: "'I'm not Nel. I'm me.
Me.' Each time she said the word *me* there was a gathering in her
like power, like joy, like fear" (24–25). Nel's assertion of selfhood, whether an indication of false pride or merely an adolescent
delusion, ends in the reality of her common identity with other
women of the community. For Sula, at least, Nel has become one
of those unindividuated women: "The narrower their lives, the
wider their hips. Those with husbands had folded themselves into
starched coffins, their sides bursting with other people's skinned
dreams and bony regrets. Those without men were like sour-
tipped needles featuring one constant empty eye" (105). In Morrison's fictions, identity is always provisional; there can be no isolated ego striving to define itself as separate from community, no
matter how tragic or futile the operations of that community
might be. Individual characters are inevitably formed by social
constructions of both race and gender, and they are inseparable
from those origins.

That early scene in *Sula* in which Shadrack attempts to discover an identity in the only mirror accessible to him, the water
in a toilet bowl, confirms the idea that "self" lies in blackness
rather than in any subjectivity or uniqueness: "There in the toilet
water he saw a grave black face. A black so definite, so unequivo-
cal, it astonished him. He had been harboring a skittish apprehen-
sion that he was not real—that he didn't exist at all. But when the
blackness greeted him with its indisputable presence, he wanted
nothing more" (11). Interestingly, in this novel, blackness is a
presence rather than an absence,[4] a key to an identity that is always
multiple, shared, a form of membership in community.[5]

Even Sula, although the novel is named for her, is not, strictly
speaking, a protagonist, for she shares the novel's focus as well as
a black identity with Nel, Shadrack, Nel's mother, Eva, and the
community itself. Her identity, multiple as it is, is a reflection of
community identity; when she absents herself from that commu-

nity for ten years, she ceases to exist within the text itself. Her much-quoted assertion, "I don't want to make somebody else. I want to make myself" (80), is almost demonic in Morrison's terms, one indication of many of the moral ambiguities Sula represents. To "make" one's self, or at least to make of one's self a single entity, is impossible, for all selves are multiple, divided, fragmented, and a part of a greater whole.

Sula's birthmark, for example, interpreted by every other character in the novel as representing a variety of images, is not only a reflection of the characters of those interpreting, but is also a valid indication of Sula's own multiplicity.[6] Her mark is, in fact, a stemmed rose, a tadpole, a snake, an ash from her mother's burning body, all interacting to represent aspects of Sula's ambiguous essence. As Deborah E. McDowell writes in "The Self and the Other: Reading Toni Morrison's *Sula* and the Black Female Text," Sula's birthmark "acts as a metaphor for her figurative 'selves,' her multiple identity" (1988, 81). McDowell concludes, based on this argument, that "Morrison's reconceptualization of character has clear and direct implications for Afro-American literature and critical study, for if the self is perceived as perpetually in process, rather than a static entity always already formed, it is thereby difficult to posit its ideal or 'positive' representation" (81). Even beyond McDowell's conception of self-in-process, however, lies the possibility of self as negation, as illusion, as contradiction, as an aspect of "the something else to be" (44) which Nel and Sula create for themselves.

Even Sula's birthmark, potentially a sign of an individual self however fragmented and multiple, is rather an indication of relationship, being one of a series of marks, brands, or emblems that Morrison employs in most of her novels, not to "distinguish" individuals, but (as blackness itself is a mark) to symbolize their participation in a greater entity, whether that is community or race or both. The marks are hieroglyphs, clues to a culture and a history more than to individual personality. Whether the "mark" is Pauline Breedlove's crippled foot in *The Bluest Eye*, Eva's missing leg in *Sula*, Pilate's navel-less stomach in *Song of Solomon*, Son's rastafarian dreadlocks in *Tar Baby*, or the crossed circle mandala branded beneath the breast of Sethe's mother in *Beloved*, or even the choke-cherry tree scars on Sethe's own back, these represent membership rather than separation. If these marks distinguish at all, they distinguish a racial identity, for most are either chosen or inflicted by the condition of blackness itself, by the poverty that has historically accompanied blackness, or by the institution of slavery which "marked" its victims literally and figuratively, physically and psychologically. "If something happens to me and you can't tell me by my face, you can know me by this mark," Sethe's African mother tells her. And the child Sethe answers, "Mark me, too . . . Mark the mark on me too" (*Beloved*, 61). Whether this is the mark of Cain or the bloodstain of a Passover, a curse or an anointment, it denotes a sisterhood (and sometimes a brotherhood as well) of Africa, which in itself is a political statement both subversive and confrontational.[7]

The verbal equivalent of such marks is the name, which, also like marks, does not necessarily designate an individual self so much as a segment of community, an identity larger than self. As Morrison has said in an interview with Thomas Le Clair: "If you come from Africa, your name is gone. It is particularly problematic because it is not just *your* name but your family, your tribe. When you die, how can you connect with your ancestors if you have lost your name? That's a huge psychological scar" (28). Of least importance in Morrison's novels are those names which are a part of the dominant signifying order, those denoting ownership, appropriation, those originating in slavery, those which deny group identity and African origins. In *Beloved*, Baby Suggs recalls her slave name as Jenny Whitlow; only as Mr. Garner delivers her into freedom can she turn and ask him, "why you all call me Jenny?" Her lack of a name—"Nothing . . . I don't call myself nothing" (141)—is testament to the "desolated center where the self that was no self made its home" (140). Baby Suggs has no "self" because she has no frame of reference by which to establish one, no family, no children, no context: "Sad as it was that she did not know where her children were buried or what they looked like if alive, fact was she knew more about them than she knew about herself, having never had the map to discover what she was like" (140).

Similarly, Paul D is one of a series of Pauls, identified alphabetically by some anonymous slaveholder, while Sixo is presumably the sixth of an analogous group.[8] Stamp Paid, born Joshua under slavery, has, however, chosen and devised his own symbolic name, which represents a rejection of a tradition of white naming as well as a celebration of freedom. His name is also and more specifically a symbol of freedom from debt; because he suffered under slavery and because he "handed over his wife to his master's son" (184), he has paid in misery any obligation to humanity, he believes, although his continued activity as a conductor on the Underground Railroad would indicate otherwise. All African Americans are, in essence, "Stamp Paid," Morrison implies.

Sethe's name is one of the few in this novel chosen by a mother, and that name is a mark of blackness and of acceptance into tribe and culture. As Nan tells the "small girl Sethe," "She threw them all away but you. The one from the crew she threw away on the island. The others from more whites she also threw away. Without names, she threw them. You she gave the name of the black man" (62). Whether this name is derived from that of the Egyptian god, Seth, or from the biblical Seth, it represents, like most of the names that Morrison designates as chosen, a sense of heritage and a context of relational identity.

And, Beloved, whose birth name we never learn, takes her identity from the single word on her tombstone and from the love her mother bears her, the paradox of which is reflected in the novel's epigraph from *Romans*: "I will call them my people, which were not my people; and her beloved, which was not beloved." Finally, Beloved has no identity other than that merged with the "Sixty million and more" of the dedication, all those who suffered the outrage of enslavement; her consciousness is a group consciousness, her memory a racial memory of the Middle Passage. All names in Morrison's fictions, finally, are, like that of Beloved, names of the "Disremembered and unaccounted for, she cannot be lost because no one is looking for her, and even if they were, how can they call her if they don't know her name?" (275).

Early in *Song of Solomon*, Macon Dead considers that he might have a better sense of the identity for which he futilely strives throughout the novel, mainly through an accumulation of wealth and an approximation of white bourgeois standards of living, if he could locate his ancestral context: "Surely, he thought, he and his sister had some ancestor, some lithe young man with onyx skin and legs as straight as cane stalks, who had a name that was real. A name given to him at birth with love and seriousness. A name that was not a joke, nor a disguise, nor a brand name" (17). For three generations, the Macon Deads have borne a name, the drunken mistake of a white bureaucrat, which is both a brand and a joke that continues throughout the novel: "You can't kill me. I'm already Dead." Although Milkman's nickname is so ignominiously earned, also a joke, and his character so ironically ambiguous, formed as it is by a parody of patriarchy, his ultimate dignity lies in his final realization of the importance of "Names that bore witness" (333).

Morrison's epigraph to the novel reads, "The fathers may soar / And the children may know their names," but it is, finally, also the names of the ancestral mothers which bear witness. Pilate's ambiguous name (inherently subversive in its anti-Christian intimations), selected by that family custom of placing a finger on the first word in an opened Bible (even though, in Pilate's case, the namer was unable to read), is so critical to her that she places the written inscription of it in a box that she wears strung through her earlobe, not because her identity as an individual is threatened, but because the name itself is a connection with family, with tradition and history. Even the young Milkman knows that Pilate's box contains the magic knowledge of all names: "Pilate knows. It's in that dumb-ass box hanging from her ear. Her own name and everybody else's" (89).

Pilate carries her name with her, just as she carries a rock from every state in which she has lived, to provide continuity in an otherwise random and dispossessed existence. Son in *Tar Baby* suffers a similar dispossession and also attempts to protect the name that will provide the only coherence he is capable of achieving:

> Oh, he had been alone so long, hiding and running so long. In eight years he'd had seven documented identities and before that a few undocumented ones, so he barely remembered his real original name himself. Actually the name most truly his wasn't on any of the Social Security cards, union dues cards, discharge papers, and everybody who knew it or remembered it in connection with him could very well be dead. Son. It was the name that called forth the true him. The him that he never lied to, the one he tucked in at night and the one he did not want to die. The other selves were like the words he spoke—fabrications of the moment, misinformation required to protect Son from harm and to secure that one reality at least. (119)

The primary significance of the name Son is, again, not to denote an individual self ("He did not always know who he was, but he always knew what he was like" [142]), but to place that self in a context of relationship: Son is a son of Africa and also a son of the American black male experience, the "Nigger Jims . . . Staggerlees and John Henrys. Anarchic, wandering, they read about their hometowns in the pages of out-of-town newspapers" (143). Like Pilate and any number of Morrison's other characters, Son is dispossessed, permanently "out-of-town," his name being his only connection with community and black tradition.

Most of the other characters in *Tar Baby* have at least two names, which Morrison indicates is symbolic of their fragmentation. Lost between the white and black worlds, Jadine is Jadine to her aunt and uncle but a more exotic Jade to the white Streets who have educated her and imbued her with their questionable values.[9] Ondine is Nanadine to Jadine, but Ondine to the Streets, just as Sydney is Sydney to the person he calls Mr. Street, years of intimacy not being sufficient to challenge racial and class protocol. Thérèse and Gideon are the generic Mary and Yardman to the Streets and, ironically, even to Ondine and Sydney, whose "superiority" as "Philadelphia Negroes" depends on such distinctions. Son at one point ponders Gideon's identity: "It bothered him that everybody called Gideon Yardman, as though he had not been mothered" (138). There is some justice in the fact that Margaret Street, white but as powerless as anyone else in her relationship to Valerian (whose name is that of a Roman emperor), also has multiple names—Margaret Lenore/Margarette—wherein lies her essence, "under the beauty, back down beneath it where her Margaret-hood lay in the same cup it had always lain in—faceless, silent and trying like hell to please" (71).

Choosing one's own name, in certain tragic cases, can also represent a rejection of race and culture. Helen Wright in *Sula*, for example, abhors the circumstances of her own birth to a Creole prostitute; in order to "be as far away from the Sundown House as possible" (15), she exchanges her name, Helene Sabat, with its exotic associations with the witch's sabbath, for the prosaic Helen Wright, with its implications of both "rightness" and "whiteness." Her recurrent advice to her daughter, "Don't just sit there, honey. You could be pulling your nose" (24), is further evidence of her discomfort with a racial identity she perceives as outside the limits of propriety and social acceptability by which she has defined (and thereby circumscribed) her life.

Pauline Breedlove in *The Bluest Eye* provides yet another example of Morrison's concern with the significance of naming. "Mrs. Breedlove" even to her husband and children, she is "Polly" to the white family for whom she works, and the diminutive name is totally appropriate in this case, for Pauline has diminished herself through her obsequious dedication to whiteness just as surely as little Pecola is diminished by her desire for blue eyes. Thus nicknames are often appropriate in Morrison's novels, denoting truths about character, revealing secrets, determining how a person is viewed by a particular community. Elihue Micah Whitcomb, also in *The Bluest Eye*, is called Soaphead Church by the community, a name mysterious to him but nevertheless reflective of his perverted sexual preference for "clean" little girls: "His sexuality was anything but lewd; his patronage of little girls smacked of innocence and was associated in his mind with cleanliness. He was what one might call a very clean old man" (132).

It is universal folklore that to know a person's name is to have power over that person, and this is the reason in Soaphead's mind that God refuses to name himself: in his letter to God, Soaphead challenges: "Is that why to the simplest and friendliest of questions: 'What is your name?' put to you by Moses, You would not say, and said instead 'I am who I am.' Like Popeye? I Yam What I Yam? Afraid you were, weren't you, to give out your name? Afraid they would know the name and then know you? Then they wouldn't fear you?" (142).

But the power greater than knowing a name is bestowing it, for the act of naming another reflects a desire to regulate and therefore to control. This is true throughout Morrison's fictions, and it is a major point of contention for feminist theorists as well; to be female, as to be black, is most often to suffer the oppression of being named by another. Monique Wittig in *Les Guérillères* uses a master/slave metaphor (which, when applied to Morrison's texts, is ironically pertinent) to protest a male naming of women: "unhappy one, men have expelled you from the world of symbols and yet they have given you names, they have called you slave, you unhappy slave. Masters, they have exercised their rights as masters. They write of their authority to accord names, that it goes back so far the origin of language itself may be considered an act of authority emanating from those who dominate" (112). Kristeva, too, repeatedly counsels women writers to avoid nouns, meaning that they should resist the temptation to authority which naming represents and realize the extent to which subjectivity is constructed through the disposition of such power.

Matriarchal power, always ambiguous in Morrison's novels, as we have seen in the preceding chapter, includes the equally ambiguous power to name, and a primary example of this is Eva in *Sula*. That Eva murders her son is an extension of the symbolic fact that she has already emasculated and rendered him infantile by calling him "Sweet Plum." Tar Baby, Morrison implies, might have lived more effectively if Eva had not ridiculed his white skin and infantilized him in the same stroke with her whimsical naming. And surely the Deweys would have been at least somewhat more individuated, perhaps even normal in stature, if Eva had not reduced them, truncated their potential, through her assignment of the same name for all three: "What you need to tell them apart for? They's all deweys" (32). Finally, the name is not even capitalized, and "them deweys" become a "trinity with a plural name" (33), indistinguishable in their appearance as in their childlike behavior. As Morrison has said in an interview with Bettye J. Parker, "Eva is a triumphant figure, one-legged or not. She's playing God. She maims people. But she says all of the important things" (255).

The African mothers, the ancestor figures as Morrison often refers to them, are the primary namers in Morrison's novels, just as they are the transmitters of culture and the inventors of language, itself the operative agency of culture. It is they who always "say the important things." However, the ancestor women are not themselves individuated any more than other characters; they represent a group consciousness, a history as well as a culture, what McKay refers to as the "ineffable qualities of blackness." McKay quotes Morrison as explaining that her characters have ancestors, not "just parents . . . but timeless people whose relationships to the characters are benevolent, instructive, and protective, . . . [and who] provide a certain kind of wisdom" (1988, 2). One aspect of that wisdom is that the self is a relative concept, decentered rather than alienated, relational rather than objectifying.

This relational self, which constitutes such an important pattern in Morrison's fictions, derives at least as much from the strong bonding among her female characters as it does from racial

identification. The biological states of pregnancy and of motherhood itself, in Morrison's terms, are experienced as a splitting of
the self; in *Beloved*, Sethe recounts her feelings to Beloved: "You
asleep on my back. Denver sleep in my stomach. Felt like I was
split in two" (202). No father, no man, can understand, according
to Sethe, that this condition is less a splitting than a spreading, a
dissolution of boundaries, an embrace of multiplicity. Of Paul D's
reaction to the murder of her child, Sethe says, "Too thick, he
said. My love was too thick. What he know about it? . . . when I
tell you you mine, I also mean I'm yours. I wouldn't draw breath
without my children" (203). Perhaps the closest we can come in
theoretical terms to understanding Morrison's rendering of motherhood is in Kristeva's argument in "Women's Time":

> Pregnancy seems to be experienced as the radical ordeal of the
> splitting of the subject; redoubling up of the body, separation
> and coexistence of the self and of an other, of nature and
> consciousness, of physiology and speech. This fundamental
> challenge to identity is then accompanied by a fantasy of total-
> ity—narcissistic completeness—a sort of instituted, socialized,
> natural psychosis. The arrival of the child, on the other hand,
> leads the mother into the labyrinths of an experience that, with-
> out the child, she would only rarely encounter: love for an
> other. Not for herself, nor for an identical being, and still less
> for another person with whom "I" fuse (love or sexual passion).
> But the slow, difficult and delightful apprenticeship in atten-
> tiveness, gentleness, forgetting oneself. (1981, 26)

Cixous, too, sees motherhood as the ultimate subversion of male-
defined subjectivity; in "The Laugh of the Medusa," she writes:
"The mother, too, is a metaphor. It is necessary and sufficient that
the best of herself be given to woman by another woman for her
to be able to love herself and return in love the body that was
'born' to her. Touch me, caress me, you the living no-name, give
me my self as myself" (313).

In Morrison's mother/daughter relationships, no Lacanian
mirror (and the separation from the mother that mirror represents) interferes with the preoedipal relationship, that sometimes
destructive yet also potentially positive arrangement which occurs
in each one of Morrison's novels and the discussion of which pervades each chapter of the present study. Most Western psycholo-
gists, including Chodorow in *The Reproduction of Mothering*, see

a possible pathology in such an arrangement: Chodorow notes those cases in which "mothers maintained their daughters in a nonindividuated state through behavior which grew out of their own ego and body-ego boundary blurring and their perception of their daughters as one with, and interchangeable with, themselves" (1978, 100). While Morrison, too, sees such boundary confusion as problematic (see Chapters 1 and 4 in particular), she nevertheless renders her female family relationships as powerfully positive agents in the lives of black women.[10] "Dread of the mother" (Chodorow 1978, 183) occurs in Morrison, too, but is always mitigated by a love that is virtually erotic, a merging of identities that transcends Western ideas about self and other, about subject and object.

Sula, for example, is primarily and inevitably one of "those Peace women" (35), linked inextricably to her mother and grandmother, with both of whom she shares personality traits and behavior patterns. Sula, like Hannah, "went to bed with men as frequently as she could" (105), and, like Eva, Sula is also a murderer, her participation in the drowning of Chicken Little almost as damning as Eva's act of burning Plum. Sula's passive pleasure in watching her mother burn—"not because she was paralyzed, but because she was interested" (67)—is no less dispassionate than Eva's self-mutilation, her sacrifice of her leg for insurance money to feed her children. Even this mutilation, the use of one's own body as sacrifice and also as political statement, is echoed by Sula's act of cutting off the tip of her finger to protect herself and Nel and to threaten the abusive boys who terrorize them. Like Eva and because of Eva, Sula has "no center, no speck around which to grow . . . no ego. For that reason she felt no compulsion to verify herself—be consistent with herself" (103). According to Cynthia Davis, it is Sula's rejection of her mother, and ultimately of Eva as well, which is that factor determining her lack of center, her "'splitting of the self,' a denial of facticity that can produce a centerless hero like Sula" (1990, 22).

The same relationship characterized by ambiguity exists in *Song of Solomon* among Pilate, Reba, and Hagar. The daughter, Reba, like Hannah in *Sula*, is relatively inconsequential, content to live obscurely in her more powerful and protective mother's shadow; the more intense relationship and more obvious doubling occurs between grandmother and granddaughter. Pilate and

Hagar form a continuum of "wildness," each a "wilderness girl," each manifesting the jungle of the female essence, like "every witch that ever rode a broom straight through the night to a ceremonial infanticide as thrilled by the black wind as by the rod between her legs" (128). Pilate's love for Hagar, finally, is more destructive and more tragic than Hagar's love for Milkman, and Hagar is "My baby girl" (322–23) to the moment of her death, locked but secure in the matriarchal realm that is her existence.

The merging of identities in the preoedipal bonding of the female triad is universal in Morrison's work but most pronounced in *Beloved*, the relationship among Baby Suggs, Sethe, and Denver giving way to that inverted trinity of Sethe, Denver, and Beloved, who become "us three," the "hand-holding shadows" on the road (182). The first thing we learn of Beloved's manifested presence at 124 Bluestone Road is the shattered mirror (3), highly significant as a prefiguration of the shattering and merging of identities that will occur throughout the novel. Even before Beloved's actual physical appearance, she is part of the trinity that represents both love and destruction, the empty white dress kneeling beside Sethe which Denver sees through the window: "The dress and her mother together looked like two friendly grown-up women—one (the dress) helping out the other" (29). But always the hands that begin with a caress end by attempting to strangle: "Putting the thumbs at the nape, while the fingers pressed the sides. Harder, harder, the fingers moved slowly around toward her windpipe, making little circles on the way. Sethe was actually more surprised than frightened to find that she was being strangled" (96). After Beloved arrives in the flesh, manifests herself on the tree stump outside 124, the three women live together, virtually at the end of the world, on the edge of consciousness and experience, sharing identity as they share the pair-and-a-half of ice skates on a mystical winter night when, repeatedly, "Nobody saw them falling" (174–75). The preoedipal bonding is also symbolized by Sethe's preparation of the "hot sweet milk" (175) they share on their return from skating.

Denver is the first to sense the melting of identity, the merging that is her love for Beloved, whose blood she has drunk "right along with my mother's milk" (205). Believing that Beloved has left her and returned to her otherworldly existence, Denver realizes "she has no self. . . . She can feel her thickness thinning, dissolving into nothing. She grabs the hair at her temples to get enough to uproot it and halt the melting for a while. . . . She doesn't move to open the door because there is no world out there" (123). Beloved, too, finds herself melting, surrealistically disintegrating, as she surprises herself by pulling out one of her own teeth:

> Beloved looked at the tooth and thought, This is it. Next would be her arm, her hand, a toe. Pieces of her would drop maybe one at a time, maybe all at once. Or on one of those mornings before Denver woke and after Sethe left she would fly apart. It is difficult keeping her head on her neck, her legs attached to her hips when she is by herself. Among the things she could not remember was when she first knew that she could wake up any day and find herself in pieces. She had two dreams: exploding, and being swallowed. When her tooth came out—an odd fragment, last in the row—she thought it was starting. (133)

Beloved is, finally, "exploded right before their eyes" (263) according to community women, but not before there has occurred a merging of voices and minds as well as of bodies: "I am Beloved and she is mine. . . . She smiles at me and it is my own face smiling. . . . Your face is mine. . . . Will we smile at me? . . . She is the laugh; I am the laughter. . . . Beloved/You are my sister/ You are my daughter/You are my face; you are me. . . . You are mine/You are mine/You are mine" (214–17). It requires all of Paul D's strength and all the power of a community of women to separate this triad, to disperse the ghost, to save Sethe's life, and to return Denver to a "real" world. Paul D, with his male energy and his love, restores Sethe to at least a kind of subjectivity; but we wonder, at the end (such is the power of Morrison's ambiguity), whether or not he is more killer than healer, whether he lies when he says: "You your best thing, Sethe. You are" (273).[11] The last word in the novel, after all, is "Beloved," relegated though she is to the dreamworld, the realm of dark water, the unconscious where the self is always split and illusory, where "the sound of one's own feet going seem to come from a far-off place" (274).

Beloved, then, is both self and other, and always, in Morrison's fictions, such dichotomies are suggested only to be invalidated, subverted, rejected. The dyad is as important imagistically and philosophically for Morrison as the triad, and doubling becomes as effective a way of questioning the concept of self as does a fragmentation of identity in the tripled preoedipal arrangement. Oppositions and polarities are created between and within the characters, but only to be blurred, obscured, and finally negated.

Shortly after Nel's discovery in the mirror of her "me-ness," she meets Sula, who dispels that claim to individuality; for Sula and Nel come to represent aspects of a common self, a construction of identity *in relationship*. "Nel was the first person who had been real to her, whose name she knew" (103), Morrison writes of this friendship cemented not only by time and proximity but by complicity, a common and recurrent recognition of the river "with a closed place in the middle," the place where Chicken Little, the male sacrifice to female power, has disappeared. For Nel, "Talking to Sula had always been a conversation with herself" (82), and, when Sula returns after Nel's marriage, "It was like getting the use of an eye back" (82).[12] Sula, too, is conscious of the power and strength that the relationship once assured for each, and she remembers "the days when we were two throats and one eye and we had no price" (126).

Although Morrison is obviously sympathetic to Nel's pain and loneliness, she nevertheless holds her more responsible for the interruption of this friendship than Sula; for, although Sula sleeps with Nel's husband,[13] Nel has broken faith by marrying him in the first place, by reordering priorities and values according to social standards and giving herself over "to the town and all of its ways" (104). Sula, on the other hand, "had no thought at all of causing Nel pain when she bedded down with Jude. They had always shared the affection of other people: compared how a boy kissed, what line he used with one and then the other" (103). Sula knows long before Nel finally realizes that "a lover was not a comrade and could never be—for a woman" (104), and that the truly relational self and the ultimate value lie in the fact that "We was girls together" (149).

Comfort with the merging of identities, however, is only possible for the women in Morrison's fictions, most of the male relationships, such as that between Milkman and Guitar in *Song of Solomon*, suffering in contrast.[14] Theirs is a brotherhood based not on intimacy and the merging of identity so much as on competition for dominance and a common need for protection in a world that is totally hostile to young black men and so preclusive of their dreams. As Railroad Tommy tells the young Guitar and Milkman, black manhood is a catalogue of thwarted dreams and frustrated desire, and the only thing they will not be denied is "a broken heart. . . . And folly. A whole lot of folly. You can count on it" (60). Guitar serves mostly as a foil for Milkman, and perhaps Melvin Dixon is correct in his observation that Guitar's very name characterizes, not latent musical ability, but his role as "instrumental in Milkman's development of character and cultural awareness" (133). Finally, however, the form of communication between Milkman and Guitar lies in violence rather than affection, a vague homoerotic attachment rathehan love. Guitar is a real threat to Milkman's very life when, in the final lines, Milkman flies, jumps, into "the killing arms of his brother" (341).

Guitar represents, however, the repressed and wild part of Milkman's self, just as Sula fulfills this role for Nel. Like Sula, and like a number of Morrison's other characters, Guitar has golden eyes, yet another kind of mark, analogous to those discussed above, which places him in a category outside that of ordinary experience and within the context of another kind of membership, here in the wild zone that is beyond the recognizably and socially acceptable area of the rational. Morrison has called her golden-eyed heroes "the salt tasters," and she sees their particular freedom as dangerous to society and to themselves, yet they are always attractive, compelling:

> They are the misunderstood people in the world. There's a wildness that they have, a nice wildness. It has bad effects in society such as the one in which we live. It's pre-Christ in the best sense. It's Eve. When I see this wildness gone in a person, it's sad. This special lack of restraint, which is a part of human life and is best typified in certain black males, is of particular interest to me. It's in black men despite the reasons society says they're not supposed to have it. . . . It's a kind of self-flagellant resistance to certain kinds of control, which is fascinating. Opposed to accepted notions of progress, the lock-step life, they live in the world unreconstructed and that's it. (Tate 1989, 125–26)

Cholly Breedlove in *The Bluest Eye*, with his "yellow eyes, flaring nostrils" (91) and his dangerous freedom, is one such character; Ajax in *Sula* is another; and so is Shadrack, "The terrible Shad who walked about with his penis out, who peed in front of

ladies and girl-children, the only black who could curse white
people and get away with it" (53). Son in *Tar Baby* also represents
nothing so much as "Wildness. Plain straight-out wildness" (165).
Sixo in *Beloved* is yet another manifestation of this same outlaw
wildness, this unrepressed jungle that is actually a part of all Morrison's people, although most of them fail to recognize it: "Sixo
went among trees at night. For dancing, he said, to keep his
bloodlines open, he said. Privately, alone, he did it. None of the
rest of them had seen him at it, but they could imagine it, and the
picture they pictured made them eager to laugh at him—in day-
light, that is, when it was safe" (25).

But, of course, there is no such thing as safety for Morrison's
wilderness characters, and they are inevitably hunted down, separated from community, or even destroyed. They are not so much
individuals as they exist in relation to a community, and their
function is most often that of pariah, their purpose ultimately the
purification of that community, as it was the biblical Cain's to be
marked and banished into the wilderness, taking with him the sins
of the world. Community for Morrison is always a force to be
reckoned with, a character itself as powerful as any individual.
Terry Otten sees this force as prescriptive, and allegiance to community as a prerequisite to survival: "In all Morrison's novels
alienation from community, or 'the village,' invariably leads to
dire consequences, and the reassertion of community is necessary
for the recovery of order and wholeness" (1989, 93). Similarly,
Keith E. Byerman defines the importance of community in *Sula* as
crucial: "It establishes the forms of male-female, parent-child,
individual-society, good-evil relationships. It creates rituals recognizing the mysteries of birth, sex, and death; it codifies acceptable attitudes toward power, whether personal, sexual, or racial.
In other words, it makes the conventions that define life in the
Bottom" (65). Morrison has written, in an essay entitled "Rootedness: The Ancestor as Foundation," "If anything I do, in the
way of writing novels or whatever I write, isn't about the village
or the community or about you, then it isn't about anything"
(Evans, 339). Morrison defines community in terms of its fictional value as a Greek chorus: commenting on the action, serving
as a guide for the reader from the "real" world into the fabulous,
making things credible. But the community in Morrison's fictions
is never benign, and like all of her characters, community itself is

morally ambiguous, comprising as it does a force for conformity, a demand for sanity, an argument for rationality—none of which qualities are totally or always desirable for either Morrison or her wilderness characters.

The "we" in *The Bluest Eye*, for example, is wider in implication than the ostensible "we" of Claudia and her sister Frieda, for Claudia speaks for community as a whole, the black community of Lorain, Ohio, but also the world community. Claudia shares in a universal guilt for a failure of tolerance, an inability to love sufficiently or to love at all. There is a distinctly malicious quality to the town gossip (to which Claudia always listens), as well as a perverse pleasure in the misfortunes and misbehaviors of the few, such as the Breedloves, whose actions, and even appearance, render them pariahs, place them outside the community and, in fact, "outdoors":

> Outdoors, we knew, was the real terror of life. The threat of being outdoors surfaced frequently in those days. Every possibility of excess was curtailed with it. If somebody ate too much, he could end up outdoors. If somebody used too much coal, he could end up outdoors. People could gamble themselves outdoors, drink themselves outdoors. . . . There is a difference between being put *out* and being put *outdoors*. If you are put out, you go somewhere else; if you are outdoors, there is no place to go. The distinction was subtle but final. Outdoors was the end of something, an irrevocable, physical fact, defining and complementing our metaphysical condition. (17–18)

According to Claudia's Mama, "that old Dog Breedlove had burned up his house, gone upside his wife's head, and everybody, as a result, was outdoors" (17). As Davis explains, "The characters who are 'outdoors,' cut off from reassuring connection and definition, are profoundly frightening to the community, especially to a community dispossessed and 'peripheral'; it responds by treating the free person as another kind of scapegoat, using that 'excess' to define its own life" (1990, 14).

The community may be justified in many ways, but not for its virtual pleasure in the fact that Cholly—already excluded by his ugliness and his poverty, having always been outdoors, outlawed, outraged and outrageous, out of control—has raped his daughter, that she gives birth to his baby, and that she goes mad in the end: "After the gossip and the slow wagging of heads. . . .

Grown people looked away; children, those who were not frightened by her, laughed outright" (158). Cholly is sufficiently fortunate to die in the workhouse, but Pecola lives on on the periphery of the community, picking through its metaphysical and
metaphorical garbage, serving, as Roberta Rubenstein writes, as
"the dark shadow, the Other, that undermines both white and
black fantasies of female goodness, beauty, and upward mobility"
(130). Pecola is necessary to her community; she cleanses and
beautifies it by her own ugliness:

> All of our waste which we dumped on her and which she ab-
> sorbed. And all of our beauty, which was hers first and which
> she gave to us. All of us—all who knew her—felt so wholesome
> after we cleaned ourselves on her. We were so beautiful when
> we stood astride her ugliness. Her simplicity decorated us, her
> guilt sanctified us, her pain made us glow with health, her awk-
> wardness made us think we had a sense of humor. Her inarticu-
> lateness made us believe we were eloquent. Her poverty kept us
> generous. Even her waking dreams we used—to silence our
> own nightmares. (159)

Surely this community and the world it represents is culpable—
mean and small and narrow. The "we" implicates the reader as
well as Claudia, for, in some mistaken but seemingly universal
need for self-definition through comparison with an Other, that
which we create and then regard as inferior, "the thing we assas-
sinated" (160) is forever our own integrity.

The community in *Sula* is not a great deal more sympathetic,
characterized primarily by the "church women who frowned on
any bodily expression of joy (except when the hand of God com-
manded it)" (68) and convinced that "the only way to avoid the
Hand of God is to get in it" (56). Here, however, there is a dignity of endurance, for this community lives for the most part no-
bly in the face of its oppressions and sorrows, and its virtue is
defined in large measure by its tolerance of Sula. Morrison has
said that she sees the community in *Sula* as "nurturing," if for no
other reason than that "There was no other place in the world she
could have lived without being harmed. Whatever they think
about Sula, however strange she is to them, however different,
they won't harm her" (Tate 1989, 130). Nurturing or not, the
community is clearly still requiring the blood sacrifice of the pa-

riah for its survival. Not "outdoors" but nonetheless outside of community, the Peace women are prime candidates, particularly Sula whose birthmark is so obvious a symbol, a mark of the beast or the rose of Christ, certainly referred to in Morrison's epigraph from Tennessee Williams's *The Rose Tattoo*: "Nobody knew my rose of the world but me. . . . I had too much glory. They don't want glory like that in nobody's heart."

It is not merely Sula's blatant sexuality and promiscuity the community abhors (they had tolerated the same behavior in Hannah), but perhaps her "glory" lies in her prettiness (which acts to separate her, much as did Pecola's ugliness) and her lack of "any normal signs of vulnerability" (100). Perhaps Sula, like most of the outsiders in Morrison's fictions, also represents an aspect of community that it does not wish to confront, namely, its own essence, its own unconscious, for Sula is a part of every member, a part of an idea of blackness itself. As Morrison describes her in "The Afro-American Presence in American Literature," she is "quintessentially black, metaphysically black, if you will, which is not melanin and certainly not unquestioning fidelity to the tribe. She is new world black and new world woman extracting choice from choicelessness. . . . Improvisational. Daring, disruptive, imaginative, modern, out-of-the-house, outlawed, unpolicing, uncontained and uncontainable" (1990, 223).

Sula is thus an intrinsic part of community just as she is a part of an idea of God. She is the Jungian shadow, that last unexplained quadrant of the crossed circle symbolic of mandelic wholeness, the fourth face of the Holy Trinity without which Father, Son, and Holy Ghost are incomplete: "in their secret awareness of Him, He was not the God of three faces they sang about. They knew quite well that He had four, and that the fourth explained Sula" (102). And, identifiable as pariah and as witch, Sula purifies the community, makes it whole, encloses the "medallion" or mandala that inspires the community's very name: "Once the source of their personal misfortune was identified, they had leave to protect and love one another. They began to cherish their husbands and wives, protect their children, repair their homes and in general band together against the devil in their midst" (102). Although the community returns to its former amorality after Sula's death, she remains for the people "the most magnificent hatred they had ever known" (148–49), making good her own deathbed prophecy: "Oh, they'll love me all right. It will take time, but they'll love me" (125).

At least one person in Medallion does love Sula; Shadrack, the Holy Fool to Sula's witch, an incarnation of the River God of African lore, is her counterpart and the recipient of a virtually mystical transferral of mission, symbolized by Sula's belt, which Shadrack keeps as a talisman, and by the exchange of a single word, one that denies death: "always." He recognizes in Sula a life principle; she is "his woman, his daughter, his friend" (135), and her female essence contradicts or at least balances his experience of war (Morrison's equivalent to the biblical fiery furnace in which the original Shadrack found his apotheosis) and his fear of death. In order to control that fear, to order death, Shadrack has instituted "Suicide Day": "If one day a year were devoted to it, everybody could get it out of the way and the rest of the year would be safe and free" (12). The community depends on the annual regularity of Shadrack's ceremonial bell-ringing and his ritual invitation to death; but it is not until just after Sula's death and their own moral backsliding has occurred that the people respond. Like the Pied Piper leading away the children of Hamlin in revenge for a bad debt, Shadrack leads a great many members of the community to their deaths in the abandoned tunnel, thus not only ordering death itself but also ridding the town of its "rats," its unconscious guilt, and thus purifying it, just as Sula has done, and Pecola and Cholly Breedlove before her.

Unless we consider the brief interlude in Eloe, Florida, there is no actual community depicted in *Tar Baby*; rather, there is a single house that is a melting pot of white and black and an island that isolates and renders this group unique in the world. But even this small number of people requires its scapegoats, its agents of purification and moral regeneration, its confrontation with the dark face of the other which is also the self. Son, manifesting himself from the sea, hiding in people's closets, shaking his dreadlocks, is, as Rubenstein suggests, "a demon from the white unconscious" (127), or, as Otten theorizes, "a serpent in paradise" (104). His function is to tear aside the veils, remove the masks that dominate as image in the novel,[15] expose the secrets of every other character, to force confrontation with "truth" in all its many manifestations. Because of Son's presence, Valerian's "innocence" is challenged and his inherent racism revealed; Margaret's deep secret that she tortured her infant son with pins and cigarette burns is exposed; Sydney and Ondine's superior but nevertheless subservient blackness is at least partially subverted; and Jadine is introduced for the first time to her own blackness, the superficiality of her choices of "Ave Maria" over gospel music and Picasso over an Itumba mask (62). She is also radically confronted with her own sexuality: "He had jangled something in her that was so repulsive, so awful, and he had managed to make her feel that the thing that repelled her was not in him, but in her" (105). By the end of the novel and Son's return to the unconscious, symbolized by the maternal swamp, L'Arbe de la Croix is in a shambles, riddled with truths, shattered, fallen, but somehow also redeemed.

No such redemption is possible for members of the black community of Cincinnati who, in *Beloved*, live furtive lives, a few short years and a few miles across the Ohio River being all that separates them from the terrors of slavery. Like Pilate's house in *Song of Solomon*, "just barely within the boundaries of the elaborately socialized world of black people" (150), Baby Suggs's house is also on the edge of community, the periphery of town, the margins of social existence. Its isolation began the day on which Sethe killed her daughter and the community deserted her, simply removing itself from the guilt it surely felt for not having warned Sethe of the slave catcher's approach, for not having sent "a fleet-footed son to cut 'cross a field soon as they saw the four horses in town hitched for watering while the riders asked questions. Not Ella, not John, not anybody ran down or to Bluestone Road, to say some new whitefolks with the Look just rode in" (157). Stamp Paid can only conclude that the community's failure lies in "like, well, like meanness—that let them stand aside, or not pay attention, or tell themselves somebody else was probably bearing the news already to the house on Bluestone Road where a pretty woman had been living for almost a month" (157). Anonymous contributions of food, left at Sethe's door years later, hardly constitute a retribution, nor does the army of community women who march on her house to exorcise the ghost with their singing. The community in *Beloved*, as in each of Morrison's novels, is no better or worse than the people who comprise it, not a single one of whom, as Baby Suggs tells her assembly in the wooded clearing, is "the blessed of the earth, its inheriting meek or its glorybound pure. . . . O my people, out yonder . . ."(88).

One is tempted to define Morrison's pariahs as separate from their communities and from the idea of community in general, to make them conform to that pattern of Western literature in which the artist/hero is portrayed as outside, above, and beyond his or her culture. For surely Morrison's pariahs are all artists, even though, like Sula, they lack an "art form" (105), or at least an art form that is approved by Western culture and definition. But when "art" itself becomes ubiquitous, pervasive, less an entity than a way of seeing and being in the world, as it does in Morrison's novels, then we begin to understand that the pariah as artist is part of the community as artist. Art itself, for Morrison, does not begin with the isolated and subjective individual expressing a unique talent, but rather with some more generous urge, some impetus that merges the artist with her or his world, and thus with community as well. For Morrison, art is an expression of black culture, a manifestation of that "precious, imaginative yet realistic gaze of black people" (1990, 226).

To be more specific is difficult, and perhaps "art," as Morrison considers it, ought always to be placed within quotation marks and defined by what it is *not*. Certainly, Jadine, who has studied "art history" at the Sorbonne, has a jaded view of art, one that precludes the value of African art, for example: "Picasso *is* better than an Itumba mask. The fact that he was intrigued by them is proof of *his* genius, not the mask-makers" (*Tar Baby*, 62). But also incorrect is that white, liberal view of black art which sees it as a reflection of a stereotypical concept of black life: "all grits and natural grace" (62), a combination of cowrie beads and Afro combs. Valerian and Margaret Street's always-absent son Michael, a "nice boy" whose mind is still in the grip of *The Little Prince*, is recalled as envisioning a business enterprise of African art and a resultant elimination of welfare status for the black artists he believes will contribute. According to Valerian (whose racial views are certainly no more progressive), Michael's "idea of racial progress is All Voodoo to the People," and Jadine agrees that he, and, by implication, other well-meaning but naive white people, want "a race of exotics skipping around being picturesque" (61). Jadine, of course, requires the same thing, threatened as she is by her own relation to blackness, as we see her in Eloe, camera intervening between her eyes and her vision, "having a ball photographing everybody. . . . 'Beautiful. . . . Fantastic. Now over here,' click click. . . . 'This way. Beautiful. Hold it. Hooooold it. Heaven,' click click click click" (216). Jadine herself, of course, is an "art object," a photographer's model who once graced the cover of *Elle* magazine, a white fantasy of blackness, and a parody of African art—diluted, depleted.

"Art," for Morrison, transcends appreciation for the African mask; rather, it is a quality of perception and the translation of that perception into language or music or color, all of which are indivisible, interrelated, synesthetic. By this definition, all of Morrison's characters, to relative degrees, are artists: tale-tellers, musicians, good cooks, conjurers. Even that least likely candidate for "artist," Pauline Breedlove in *The Bluest Eye*, deprived and finally depraved, is an artist in her soul, defining the world by its colors, its rainbows and its "streaks of green," and searching for order in the chaos of her experience:

> She liked, most of all, to arrange things. To line things up in rows—jars on shelves at canning, peach pits on the step, sticks, stones, leaves. . . . Whatever portable plurality she found, she organized into neat lines, according to their size, shape, or gradations of color. Just as she would never align a pine needle with the leaf of a cottonwood tree, she would never put the jars of tomatoes next to the green beans. . . . She missed—without knowing what she missed—paints and crayons. (88–89)

Pauline is like Sula, who "Had she paints, or clay, or knew the discipline of the dance, or strings; had she anything to engage her tremendous curiosity and her gift for metaphor, she might have exchanged the restlessness and preoccupation with whim for an activity that provided her with all she yearned for" (105). Pilate, too, is an artist in *Song of Solomon*, conjuring her world, brewing her wine, singing her spontaneous songs, telling her stories in magical ways, cooking her perfect eggs.

And every character in *Beloved* searches for color—and finds it in a colorless/meaningless world: "Winter in Ohio was especially rough if you had an appetite for color. Sky provided the only drama, and counting on a Cincinnati horizon for life's principal joy was reckless indeed" (4). According to Morrison, "The painterly language of *Song of Solomon* was not useful to me in *Beloved*. There is practically no color whatsoever in its pages, and when there is, it is so stark and remarked upon, it is virtually raw. Color seen for the first time, without its history" (1990, 229).

The orange square on Baby Suggs's otherwise colorless quilt and her recurring request for color in the abstract, "lavender . . . if you got any. Pink, if you don't" (4), Amy Denver's quest for "carmine" velvet, even Sethe's refusal to remember the painful life of color—"It was as though one day she saw red baby blood, another day the pink gravestone chips, and that was the last of it" (39)—all are indications of the artistic vision that can see color in a colorless world and *make* life meaningful even when historical events are so antagonistic as to invalidate aesthetic consideration.

Finally, it is Denver who will reinvent color and retell Sethe's stories, for art survives in spite of history. Denver is also Morrison's symbol for hope, for the bridge between alienation and community, for the survival of identity, associated as that always is with both race and gender. Along with Lady Jones, we look at Denver in the wildly colored clothes in which Sethe has dressed her with the recognition that "Everybody's child was in that face" (246).

3

"The Disremembered and Unaccounted For": History, Myth, and Magic

> You say you have lost all recollection of it, remember. . . . You say there are no words to describe this time, you say it does not exist. But remember. Make an effort to remember. Or failing that, invent.
>
> —Monique Wittig, *Les Guérillères*

Just as she reinscribes femininity and identity, Toni Morrison reinscribes a history that is less individual than racial and national; hers is also a psychic and a mythic history, a feminine subtext, the kind Cixous and Clément describe in *The Newly Born Woman* as "a history, taken from what is lost within us of oral tradition, of legends and myths—a history arranged the way tale-telling women tell it" (6).

All of Morrison's novels are, in a real sense, "historical novels," quasi documentaries that bear historical witness. Her characters are both subjects *of* and subject *to* history, events in "real" time, that succession of antagonistic movements that includes slavery, reconstruction, depression, and war. Yet she is also concerned with the interaction of history with art, theory, and even fantasy, for, in her terms, history itself may be no more than a brutal fantasy, a nightmare half-remembered, in which fact and symbol become indistinguishable. As we have seen in previous chapters, Morrison always moves beyond the dimensions of the given, beyond the recording of fact, into an area that is at the edge of consciousness and experience, an area Jardine in *Gynesis* defines

61

as "neither Reality, nor History, nor a Text. The Real dissipates that which is categorically unrepresentable, non-human, at the limits of the known; it is emptiness, the scream, the 'zero-point' of death . . . " (567).

Had it not been 1941, stated but also symbolized by the presence of a little white girl sitting in "a 1939 Buick eating bread and butter" that she refuses to share (*The Bluest Eye*, 12), Pecola Breedlove might not have undergone the extremities of poverty dictated by her depression epoch. Poverty, the way Morrison renders it, is a historical fact, documented by the necessity to gather coal along railroad tracks, by the "tired, edgy voices" of adults, by the persistence of mice and roaches, and by the hellish orange glow of steel mills in Lorain, Ohio (12). But, for Morrison, poverty is also a *place*, a state of being, a frame of mind, and its effects are catastrophic, taking their toll in human dignity and self-respect, finally even in sanity.

Ironically juxtaposed to the primary-school-reader vision of the pretty green house with the red door where Dick and Jane live with the smiling mother and the big father, Pecola's house is an abandoned store, a "gray box" that "does not recede into its background of leaden sky" but "foists itself on the eye of the passerby in a manner that is both irritating and melancholy" (30). And we also know intimately the interior of this house, which comes to signify all houses that manifest poverty: the coal stove, which is the only "living thing," and the furniture itself, which has been "conceived, manufactured, shipped, and sold in various states of thoughtlessness, greed, and indifference" (31). There is no bathroom, no privacy, no dignity; human energy is depleted on things that do not function. These are the facts on which the novel is based, dictated by the time in which it is set. But time is also rendered figuratively, poetically, like coats of paint, its passage recorded in the manner of "tale-telling women," its existence relegated to the realm of myth: "probably no one remembers longer, longer ago, before the time of the gypsies and the time of the teen-agers when the Breedloves lived there, nestled together in the storefront. Festering together in the debris of a realtor's whim" (31). Hysteria, Freud wrote, is a matter of *place*, but he might well have added that it is also a matter of *time*.

History, as well as hysteria, is, in Morrison's fictions, always a matter of both time and place. Ohio as a frequent setting occurs not only because she was born in Lorain but because of that state's significance in the history of African Americans. Morrison has said in an interview that

> Ohio is a curious juxtaposition of what was ideal in this country and what was base. It was also a Mecca for black people; they came to the mills and plants because Ohio offered the possibility of a good life, the possibility of freedom, even though there were some terrible obstacles. Ohio also offers an escape from stereotyped black settings. It is neither plantation nor ghetto. (Tate 1989, 119)

Locale is always deeply and historically significant for Morrison, whether the place is Lorain, Ohio, with its orange glow of the steel mills; or Milkman's Detroit, the Motown of the industrial north in *Song of Solomon*; or postslavery Cincinnati in *Beloved*, where life for black people centers around the pig yards:

> Cincinnati was still pig port in the minds of Ohioans. Its main job was to receive, slaughter and ship up the river the hogs that Northerners did not want to live without. . . . The craving for pork was growing into a mania in every city in the country. Pig farmers were cashing in, provided they could raise enough and get them sold farther and farther away. And the Germans who flooded southern Ohio brought and developed swine cooking to its highest form. Pig boats jammed the Ohio River. . . . (154–55)

Morrison's most exotic setting is Isle des Chevaliers in *Tar Baby*, literally at "the end of the world" (7) from Ohio; here, in the Caribbean, color, like life itself, is intense: "The island exaggerated everything. Too much light. Too much shadow" (57). But, like Cincinnati or like Lorain, even this gorgeous place, "the shore of an island that, three hundred years ago, had struck slaves blind the moment they saw it" (5), is founded on the backs of black laborers and the exploitation of human resources by white capitalists; in its modern configuration, Isle des Chevaliers is still a forum for racial tension, a link in the chain of black history that is synonymous with oppression.

Morrison's geography, urban though it usually is, inevitably includes a sense of the natural world, an indication that the passage of time has significance beyond the conception of recorded history. *The Bluest Eye*, for example, is ordered by the presentation of a series of rooms or interior spaces, but also by the passage of seasons from autumn to summer, the way a child perceives such passage, what Morrison refers to as "seasons in childtime" (1990, 220). Just as she ironically contrasts the white myth of the Dick and Jane reader with the reality of Pecola's life, so Morrison contrasts the great fertility myth of the seasons to the irony that marigolds won't grow in Lorain, Ohio, and that Pecola ends by spending her "sap green days, walking up and down, up and down, her head jerking to the beat of a drummer so distant only she could hear" (158). As is true in all of her novels, Morrison juxtaposes the natural order with the failure of human social order. The last image we have of Pecola is also one of ironic contrast: she haunts the narrator and the reader with her perpetual existence "on the edge of my town," which is also the edge of community, of culture, "among the garbage and the sunflowers" (160). Pecola exists because of, within, and beyond history, a testament to society's denial of responsibility and its failure to love what it chooses not to see.

Sula, too, is a historical novel, its events carefully recorded within the context of specific years that are significant because they either denote or, even more powerfully, *suggest* the reality of war. As Maureen T. Reddy has discovered, the prologue to the novel recalls the Civil War in its legend about the "Nigger joke" of the freed slave whose master gives him "bottom" land at the top of the rocky hills surrounding the mythical Medallion, Ohio. The next section, "1919," recounts the terrors of World War I as perceived through the consciousness of a single soldier, Shadrack, who is driven mad by the carnage he witnesses and whose presence, and therefore that of World War I, permeates the rest of the novel; another section is titled "1941," suggesting but not documenting yet another war; and the merest mention of the date "1965" in the epilogue implies the reality of Vietnam. As Reddy remarks, *Sula* is "a war novel, or, more precisely, an anti-war novel," and "Peace" is not only Sula's last name but an ironic observation on the historical lack of any such thing (30).

While the characters of *Sula*, like those in other of Morrison's novels, are victims of history, they are not, somehow, prisoners of time, for they live simultaneously in memory and dreams and in the sense of a future—however apocalyptic, however ironically redemptive—a future, as Sula recites on her deathbed, "when all the black men fuck all the white ones; when all the white women kiss all the black ones; when the guards have raped all the jailbirds and after all the whores make love to their grannies . . . when Lindbergh sleeps with Bessie Smith and Norma Shearer makes it with Stepin Fetchit" (125). Time in Morrison's works is always arbitrary, circular rather than linear. Even death, that necessary effect of time, can be transcended, as Sula lives on after death to change the lives of her community and manifest herself to Nel years later in the rustling of leaves: "'Sula?' she whispered, gazing at the tops of trees. 'Sula?'" (149). As Morrison said in an interview with Parker, "She doesn't stop existing after she dies. In fact, what she left behind is more powerful after she is dead than when she was alive" (254).

Ghosts, both actual and figurative, from a past that is both historic and mythic, also dominate the actions of all the characters in *Song of Solomon*, all of whom resurrect their fathers and seek the meaning of the present in the legends of the past. Morrison dedicates this book to "Daddy," and her epigraph reads, "The fathers may soar / And the children may know their names." The quest of Milkman Dead, assigned to him, in part, by his father, is ostensibly a quest for gold and for a personal history, a racial identity, which he believes will be realized only in the context of the ancestral fathers. As Genevieve Fabre documents, *Song of Solomon* is a literary example of genealogical archaeology:

> Its drifting and uninformed hero is caught in the ambiguities of a quest that presents itself as a succession of riddles; each recorded incident, act, or word is a new adventure that further complicates the overall puzzle. And the legacy—an ever elusive reality—takes on many serious or trivial forms: a name, a birthmark, a bag of bones, or a song. Each is presented as a possible clue or a new mystery. The deciphering of the enigma is seen as a game in which the character and the reader are jostled from one puzzle to the next. Answers are presented piece by piece through hints that create further suspense, and this accounts for the structure of this enigmatic narrative: a pattern of revelation and deception, or recognition and denial. (107–8)

However, as Fabre also indicates, history as science, as archaeology, is merely a game, the serious aspect of knowledge remaining, not in Milkman's rediscovery of a personal history, the source of which is Solomon and his flight back to Africa, but in Pilate's wisdom and her racial memory, her intrinsically African identity, indicated on page one where she is literally cloaked in the quilt of African tradition. Hers is a female way of knowing and interpreting the significance of history. It is *she* who resolves the quest, brings Milkman to knowledge (or at least a ray of enlightenment), and who teaches him to fly, or at any rate to acknowledge that flight, in a metaphoric sense although not in any historic one, is the prerogative of women. As even Macon Dead, who is farther from his ancestors and the values they represent than any other character in the novel, can intuit: "If you ever have a doubt we from Africa, look at Pilate" (54).

Tar Baby, like *Song of Solomon*, is set in a contemporary world, but, also like *Song of Solomon*, its focus is historic and its goal the rediscovery of an African past, lost through slavery and perhaps irretrievable except through myth, and then only at the risk of life and sanity. Isle des Chevaliers is now a white man's version of paradise, but it was once a two-thousand-year-old rain forest, "scheduled for eternity" (7), the memory of which is preserved in the pervasive and indomitable swamp and in the reported but undocumented presence of a race of blind horsemen who live there, descendants of those slaves mentioned earlier who "went blind the minute they saw Dominique" (130). Son, an avatar of the ancient world and a spiritual brother to the mythological horsemen, is as lost and confused in his modern world as Milkman is in his. And, like Milkman, Son requires a guide into the realm of myth; it is Gideon who tells Son the legend, but it is Thérèse, the ancient conjure woman, herself a descendant of the blind slaves, who sends him, finally, to his spiritual kinsmen:

> Hurry. . . . They are waiting. . . . The men are waiting for you. . . . They are waiting in the hills for you. They are naked and they are blind too. I have seen them; their eyes have no color in them. But they gallop; they race those horses like angels all over the hills where the rain forest is, where the champion daisy trees still grow. Go there. Choose them. (263)

Thérèse herself is the swamp-haunt, and—like Pilate and the ageless Circe in *Song of Solomon*, like Eva Peace and Ajax's "conjure woman" mother in *Sula*, like the healer M'Dear who presides over birth and death in *The Bluest Eye*, and like the wise Baby Suggs in *Beloved*—she is also the ancestor figure, the guide through a history that transcends recorded fact, the escapee from slavery, the remnant of Africa, the keeper of racial memory, the teller of tales, often the practitioner of voodoo; and she is also an embodiment of a female principle, a way of knowing that transcends the onto-logical. Morrison's conjure women live always on the edge of both black and white cultures, relegated and sometimes confined to the wild zone, their magical powers thus contained but never completely dissipated. Always in Morrison's novels, the "edge of culture," the "wild zone" just outside of and beyond history, is the province of women, mythic figures who are not themselves actors in history but necessary mediators between biology and history, conservators of myth.

Son, with his fearsome dreadlocks and his haunted past, is the son of Africa and of his ancestors; all he needs is the passage that Thérèse provides him. Jadine/Jade, however, is an orphan daughter, separated from her African history as well as from a female way of knowing. As Thérèse tells Son, "she has forgotten her ancient properties" (263). Yet, the ancestor women manifest themselves to her; they appear in dreams or in supermarkets; they carry snow-white eggs in "tar-black fingers" (39) (Pilate also gives to Milkman a perfect egg, again symbolic of female power), wear yellow robes and colored sandals, have eyes "whose force has burnt away their lashes" (39). They are transcendently beautiful, and they represent to Jadine "that woman's woman—that mother / sister / she" (39). Sometimes they hang from trees in the swamp, watching Jadine with disapproval—quiet, arrogant, "mindful as they were of their value, their exceptional femaleness; knowing as they did that the first world of the world had been built with their sacred properties" (157). These women have no tolerance for Ja-dine, who has compromised the ancient knowledge; they spit at her, chastise her, become the "night women" who thrust their withered breasts at her "like weapons" (225); they are "the dias-pora mothers with pumping breasts" who "with a single glance from eyes that had burned away their own lashes, could discredit your elements" (248). These are the women who surge from the unconscious, more terrifying than history itself, for they represent a *lost* history, a racial identity retrievable only by a dangerous jour-ney to the mother space, which is the area of unbearable dreams and incomprehensible myths, a dark continent of the mind.

Unlike Jadine, Sethe of *Beloved* does not choose her separation from the African mother who, in this novel, is also the literal mother, removed from her daughter by the historical fact of slavery, recognizable only as a bent back and a straw hat in a distant field. Hers is the lost language and the lost heritage which surface from Sethe's unconscious only on occasion in the forms of an image or a word; Sethe considers that her unborn baby bucks like an antelope, an image she later links with the ancestor figures, shadow dancers in her own foggy past and that of her race: "Oh but when they sang. And oh but when they danced and sometimes they danced the antelope. The men as well as the ma'ams, one of whom was certainly her own. They shifted shapes and became something other. Some unchained, demanding other whose feet knew her pulse better than she did. Just like this one in her stomach" (31). Sethe's connection in the present to the ancient myths and the African mothers is through Baby Suggs, herself a conjurer who is magic and prescient but also practical. To the people who gather in her clearing to hear her "call," she gives a history and the wisdom that "the only grace they could have was the grace they could imagine. That if they could not see it, they would not have it" (88). Baby Suggs spends her dying days looking for color and for meaning, depressed and worn out and hopeless. Like Sethe, she has lost sons and daughters; of her little girl she remembers only that "she loved the burned bottom of bread. Her little hands I wouldn't know em if they slapped me" (176).

The brutal realities of history are, in this novel, more antagonistic to the psychic realm of the mother than in any other of Morrison's works. The disintegration of family, the denial of a mother's right to love her daughter, Morrison reiterates, is perhaps the greatest horror of the black experience under slavery. The final insult, the ultimate cruelty, that causes Sethe to flee Sweet Home is not the beating that results in her choke-cherry tree scars, her own brand that links her to the mothers of Africa, but the act of Schoolteacher's nephews "taking her milk," the milk meant for her "crawling-already baby." Thus the white masters not only violate Sethe in an act comparable to rape, but they also violate the sacred state of motherhood and the African spiritual values which, for Morrison, that state represents. According to Holloway and Demetrakopoulos in *New Dimensions of Spirituality*, much of Morrison's work embodies "a celebration of African archetypes" (160), the most significant of which is the Great Mother, the giver of both life and wisdom, who is *nommo*, the creative potential and the sacred aspect of nature itself. But only in freedom can Sethe celebrate her love for her children, her sense of herself as Great Mother: "It felt good. Good and right. I was big . . . and deep and wide and when I stretched out my arms all my children could get in between" (162).

Sethe and many of the other women in Morrison's novels are, like the Great Mother, metaphorically linked with images of trees and are thus representatives of the powers of nature, no matter how subverted those powers might be by circumstance or the realities of history. Like Sula, who can change the weather and identifies herself with the redwood tree, like Pilate who smells like pine trees and who can defy gravity and teach men to fly, and like the mystical women who hang from the swamp trees in *Tar Baby*, Sethe manifests power that transcends ordinary nature. Baby Suggs, too, is "holy," a magic healer who can salve the choke-cherry on Sethe's back and bind the violated breasts. She is able to conjure a feast for ninety people from two buckets of blackberries, thus rivaling the miraculous powers of the mythic Christ, and to summon the spirits that pervade the forest clearing where she calls. Hers is "the heart that pumped out love, the mouth that spoke the Word" (180). Pilate in *Song of Solomon* also manifests a love that mothers the world; her dying words to Milkman testify to a spirit that negates the atrocities of history: "I wish I'd a knowed more people. I would of loved 'em all. If I'd a knowed more, I would a loved more" (340).

Also like nature, the ultimate power of which is greater than that of history, the African Great Mother can kill as well as create; she is Kali as well as Demeter, and, as is evident in every chapter of this study, the image of the "phallic mother" is always problematic for Morrison. While she represents enduring and infinite love, the mother/ancestor is simultaneously what Cixous and Clément have defined as "The Virago, the woman with sperm," who "has a tongue that foams" (106). The Great Mother resolves polarities of creativity and destruction. As Eva Peace embraces her son before she sets him on fire in *Sula*, as Pilate Dead almost literally loves her granddaughter Hagar to death in *Song of Solomon*, so Sethe in *Beloved* takes a saw to her daughter's throat because "The best thing she was, was her children. Whites might dirty *her* all right, but not her best thing, her beautiful, magical best thing—that part of her that was clean" (151).

Sethe's mother-love is so strong that, like Demeter, she can also reverse history, resurrect that daughter, bring her back from dark water as tall and "thunderblack and glistening" (261), an image of Africa itself. According to Wilfred Cartey in "Africa of My Grandmother's Singing," within the African view of nature, "nothing is dead, no voice is still. An essential continuity is pre-served between earth-mother and child" (quoted by Holloway and Demetrakopoulos, 118). And, as was discussed in Chapter 2, Beloved is an aspect of Sethe's self and of her lost heritage, but she is also the incarnation of the "Sixty Million and more" of the novel's dedication, victims of the effectively genocidal campaign that was slavery.

But the African Great Mother is muted through slavery and the political realities of history, her powers relegated to the natu-ral rather than the political; and, for Morrison, this is an ambigu-ous qualification. Sethe is surely the victim, the image of woman as token of economic exchange rather than as a figure of glory, as she buys the engraving on Beloved's gravestone with her body, "rutting among the headstones with the engraver. . . . That should certainly be enough. Enough to answer one more preacher, one more abolitionist and a town full of disgust" (5). Pilate, too, com-mits a similar act of prostitution in *Song of Solomon*, not the sale of her body but the exchange of her integrity for Milkman's free-dom, as she transforms herself, witchlike, into Aunt Jemima in the police station: "Now, is that voluntary slavery or not?" Guitar asks, and we agree, for a moment, that "She slipped into those Jemima shoes cause they fit" (226). Helen Wright's smile at the white train conductor in *Sula*, and her resultant transformation into "custard pudding" (24), is further evidence of the political victimization of women. Through her very mythological status, the stereotype reflected in her image, woman in all of Morrison's texts is rendered a victim, a study in powerlessness within the context of a history that does not value her kind of wisdom.

In spite of the fact that Sethe's language is that of the mother, the tale-telling woman, she has no way to speak with political effectiveness, no power to change her own condition, let alone that of the world. Perhaps, as was also discussed in Chapter 1, this is partly Morrison's motivation to have Sethe act/speak with her body, to commit that one politically significant act—the mur-der of her own child—which translates the body into the word, establishes her place in history, and serves to document the nature of the most brutal of realities, to indict slavery as an institution, for, as Paul D knows, "there was no way in hell a black face could appear in a newspaper if the story was about something anybody wanted to hear" (155).

Along with other critics, Marilyn Sanders Mobley has noted, in "A Different Remembering: Memory, History, and Meaning in Toni Morrison's *Beloved*," that Sethe has her origin in "real" history (193), that she is Morrison's reinscription of Margaret Garner, a runaway slave from Kentucky whose act of infanticide was a subject for abolitionist publications at the time and is still a reminder of the atrocity that was slavery. Mobley also relates that Morrison published *The Black Book* in 1974, a collection of documents including news clippings, bills of sale, and other evidence pertaining to African American history, a historical record which Morrison felt necessary to correct what Mobley calls "a romanticization of both the African past and the American past that threatened to devalue 300 years of black life . . . as 'lived' experience" (190). But, of course, Morrison herself romanticizes the African past in *Beloved* as in other novels, inscribing it as myth and reclaiming it as part of African American identity, although her ethical position in regard to a lost Africa is always one of ironic qualification; the myth of the African Great Mother, for example, is used, not as an ideal of redemption, but as a reminder that history is the antagonist which has silenced myth, subverted nature, and dispossessed the African American of the crucial link with Africa.

Nor were Africans the only victims of dispossession and the genocidal inclinations apparently peculiar to white men in American history. Native Americans, too, are deeply symbolic for Morrison, and they haunt the pages of *Beloved* as their mythic presence does the streets of Cincinnati, where their ancient burying places are "as old as sky, rife with the agitation of dead Miami no longer content to rest in the mounds that covered them . . . they growled on the banks of Licking River, sighed in the trees on Catherine Street and rode the wind above the pigyards" (155). In his desperate escape from the inhumanities of the chain gang in Alfred, Georgia, Paul D happens upon a camp of sick and renegade Cherokee "for whom a rose was named":

> Decimated but stubborn, they were among those who chose a fugitive life rather than Oklahoma. The illness that swept them now was reminiscent of the one that had killed half their num-

ber two hundred years earlier. In between that calamity and this, they had led Oglethorpe through forests, helped Andrew Jackson fight Creek, cooked maize, drawn up a constitution, petitioned the King of Spain, been experimented on by Dartmouth, established asylums, wrote their language, resisted settlers, shot bear and translated scripture. All to no avail. The forced move to the Arkansas River, insisted upon by the same president they fought for against the Creek, destroyed another quarter of their already shattered number.

That was it, they thought, and removed themselves from those Cherokee who signed the treaty, in order to retire into the forest and await the end of the world. (111)

Only Sixo, himself soon to experience "the end of the world," respects their sacred suffering, asking their deserted structure for permission to enter and showing reverence for "the Redmen's Presence" (24).

Native Americans as the victims of history and the ghosts of myth are also a presence in *Song of Solomon*, and it is a part of Milkman's moral regeneration that he realizes the myth they represent. The immediate connection is with his grandmother, Sing Byrd, whose original identity may well have been Native American and her actual name Singing Bird. But the more important association is not personal but racial, the recognition that African Americans share with Native Americans a heritage of dispossession: "Ohio, Indiana, Michigan were dressed up like the Indian warriors from whom their names came. Blood red and yellow, ocher and ice blue. . . . The Algonquins had named the territory he lived in Great Water, *michi gami*. How many dead lives and fading memories were buried in and beneath the names of the places in this country?" (333).

Most of Morrison's characters, including Sixo, who mocks his white lynchers with the only laughter of his life, hold the white race as a whole responsible for the historic subjugation of people of color, whether it is the white farmer who perpetrates the "Nigger joke" in *Sula*, the social workers and church ladies who are so patronizing in *The Bluest Eye*, the businessmen whom Macon Dead strives so urgently to imitate to his own psychic destruction in *Song of Solomon*, the pseudoliberals and self-appointed white fathers like Valerian Street in *Tar Baby*, and—perhaps most of all—the slave owners, like Mr. Garner in *Beloved*, who see themselves as benevolent patrons, permitting manhood but denying the expression of it. According to Guitar in *Song of Solomon*, the actions of the Seven Days, exacting revenge on whites in retaliation for the crimes perpetrated on blacks, are totally justifiable. He does not kill "people," he explains, but "white people," Hitler being "the most natural white man in the world" (156).

The possible exception to this general indictment is Amy Denver, she of "the good hands," who delivers Sethe's baby and saves her life in *Beloved*. She, too, is an escapee in flight from indentured servitude and has endured her own share of oppression; that fact and her apparent limitation of intelligence act to absolve her of responsibility for what her race has perpetrated. But Sethe knows, in general, "That anybody white could take your whole self for anything that came to mind. Not just work, kill, or maim you, but dirty you. Dirty you so bad you couldn't like yourself anymore" (151). Beloved, for another, has good reason to dread "the men without skin," for their arrival is the moment of her death. Baby Suggs, too, repeatedly comments: "There is no bad luck in the world but whitefolks" (89). The Ku Klux Klan infects even the free world that Sethe believes for a time she has found: "Desperately thirsty for black blood, without which it could not live, the dragon swam the Ohio at will" (66). And Stamp Paid, who carries with him a red ribbon found on the banks of the Ohio, a red ribbon "knotted around a curl of wet wooly hair, clinging still to its bits of scalp" (180), can reflect:

> Eighteen seventy-four and whitefolks were still on the loose. Whole towns wiped clean of Negroes; eighty-seven lynchings in one year alone in Kentucky; four colored schools burned to the ground; grown men whipped like children; children whipped like adults; black women raped by the crew; property taken, necks broken. He smelled skin, skin and hot blood. The skin was one thing, but human blood cooked in a lynch fire was a whole other thing. . . . What *are* these people? You tell me, Jesus. What *are* they? (180)

Morrison fragments black history into symbols the color of blood: the choke-cherry scars on Sethe's back, Stamp Paid's piece of red ribbon, Paul D's loss of "a red, red heart," in order to tell the story of "the people of the broken necks, of fire-cooked blood and black girls who had lost their ribbons" (181). Thus does Morrison bear historical witness and redeem her muted African mothers.

Because of what she has endured from history, and because

of what it has cost her, Sethe spends her present "beating back the past" (73), her eyes "two open wells that did not reflect firelight" (9), their "iron" extinguished by unimaginable sights and the inescapable reality of "rememories." The rememories are surely intended to denote a form of racial memory, a knowledge which even future generations cannot escape or forget. Morrison has written that there is "no time" in *Beloved*, "especially no time because memory, pre-historic memory, has no time" (1990, 229). Sethe tells her daughter about the nature of time, the psychic law, not that history repeats itself, but that it exists as a place, a dimension, in the collective unconscious:

> Some things you forget. Other things you never do. . . . Places, places are still there. If a house burns down, it's gone, but the place—the picture of it—stays, and not just in my rememory, but out there, in the world. What I remember is a picture float-ing around out there outside my head. I mean, even if I don't think it, even if I die, the picture of what I did, or knew, or saw is still out there. Right in the place where it happened. . . . Someday you be walking down the road and you hear some-thing or see something going on. So clear. And you think it's you thinking it up. A thought picture. But no. It's when you bump into a rememory that belongs to somebody else. Where I was before I came here, that place is real. It's never going away. Even if the whole farm—every tree and every grass blade of it dies. The picture is still there and what's more, if you go there—you who never was there—if you go there and stand in the place where it was, it will happen again; it will be there for you, waiting for you. So, Denver, you can't never go there. Never. (36)

Beloved, who, thanks to her mother, has never been a slave and who, murdered at the age of two, has no personal memory, nevertheless retains a psychic racial memory of capture and trans-port, of slave ships and the Middle Passage. It is Morrison's nov-elistic genius which dictates that these memories be thought or spoken by Beloved herself in concert with Sethe, as their identities and their racial memories become one, in an elliptical, frag-mented, and purely poetic sequence of images. That which is too raw, too cruel, must be rendered sparingly, imagistically, and "how can I say things that are pictures" (210). The pictures them-selves are unbearable, a series of almost cinematic clips which document that human beings were packed in layers in the hold of a ship: "I am always crouching   the man on my face is dead . . . someone is thrashing but there is no room to do it in"; that extreme hunger and thirst led to the necessity to consume human excrement: "some who eat nasty themselves   I do not eat   the men without skin bring us their morning water to drink   we have none . . . if we had more to drink we could make tears   we cannot make sweat or morning water so the men without skin bring us theirs   one time they bring us sweet rocks to suck . . . in the beginning we could vomit   now we do not   now we cannot" (210). Rape and death, rats and starvation—the memories are so traumatic and so graphic that we accept with Morrison that they must persist to become universally shared, cosmically experienced.

Sethe says that it is hard for her to "believe" in time (35), and for her, as well as other of Morrison's characters, time is not linear; history is only "recovered time," stratified, circular, like language, as was discussed in Chapter 1. Sixo, for example, exists outside time in the same way that many of Morrison's women do: "Time never worked the way Sixo thought, so of course he never got it right" (21). Whether it is cooking potatoes or planning his night visits to the Thirty-Mile Woman, Sixo's time-lapse mentality provides some of the only humor in the novel. For Sethe, however, "tomorrow" is a concept too painful to consider: "Today is always here," she tells Denver. "Tomorrow, never" (60). It is deeply significant, for example, that when Sethe is recounting her past in an attempt to justify to Paul D the murder of her child, she moves about the room in circles, knowing that "the circle she was making around the room, him, the subject, would remain one. That she could never close in, pin it down for anybody who had to ask. If they didn't get it right off—she could never explain" (163).

Particularly when women live communally without men, as is the case in all five of Morrison's novels, they operate outside of history and outside of the dominant culture, even outside of black culture. Perhaps because history as a progression has been so antagonistic, they live also on a different time scheme, without schedules, without clocks, eating and sleeping according to whim or to nature rather than sanctioned custom, thus collapsing conventional temporal coherence. The three whores in *The Bluest Eye*, despite their historically significant names—China, Poland, and the Maginot Line—live outside of history and distort time itself, turning night into day; Pilate in *Song of Solomon*, and her daughter and granddaughter, live "pretty much as though progress was a word that meant walking a little farther on down the road" (27); Nel in *Sula* prefers the timelessness in Sula's "wooly house, where a pot of something was always cooking on the stove; where the mother, Hannah, never scolded or gave directions; where all sorts of people dropped in; where the newspapers were stacked in the hallway, and dirty dishes left for hours at a time in the sink, and where a one-legged grandmother named Eva handed you goobers from deep inside her pockets or read you a dream" (25). Morrison's women seem always to operate on what Kristeva has called "women's time," that arrangement of existence which refutes the value of "production" in the interest of "*reproduction*, survival of the species, life and death, the body, sex and symbol" (1981, 22).

If time and philosophy are thus inverted, then the concept of history as a linear projection is also inverted, and subverted as well. In Morrison's works, history exists as it is recalled, in fragments and pieces. Morrison's technique, thus, is to render history through the aesthetic image, to accomplish what Kristeva, in *Desire in Language*, has described as a process of the "desubstantification" of "mythic idealities, reconstructed like crystals from the practice of subjects in history" (103). This, for Kristeva, and I think for Morrison as well, is a political act, a technique that challenges the primacy of Western philosophy. Morrison provides us with the untold story, the other side of history, the reinscription of both myth and fact. Hortense Spiller sees the importance of rewriting and changing concepts of history: "Women must seek to become their own historical subject in pursuit of its proper object, its proper and specific expression in time. . . . Through the discipline and decorum exacted by form, the woman's reality is no longer a negation, but a positive and dynamic expressiveness—a figure against a field—shaped by her own insistence" (1979, 105).

Morrison's purpose in both the style and the subject of her histories is not only to invert time and disrupt chronology, but also to shock her reader into a political awareness, to challenge not only attitudes about African Americans and women but about patterns of thinking and systems of belief in general: "If my work is to confront a reality unlike that received reality of the West, it must centralize and animate information discredited by the West— discredited not because it is not true or useful or even of some racial value, but because it is information described as 'lore' or 'magic' or 'sentiment'" (Evans, 388).

Certainly there is no "sentiment" in Morrison's subjects them- selves, which are often violent, always disquieting, and sometimes almost unbearable to consider. Partly because her subjects are based on historical fact and have their origins in "reality," hers is a voice of political conscience, making poverty, slavery, oppres- sion immediate even to those readers who have never experienced them, even to those readers who would choose to forget. Morri- son thus challenges what psychiatrist Robert Jay Lifton has de- fined, in his work with survivors of the Jewish holocaust, Hiro- shima, and Vietnam, as a modern cultural "psychic numbness." According to Lifton,

> The problem is less repression of death than an impairment in the general capacity to create viable forms around it, [to bring] imagination to bear upon the unpalatable existential-historical truths, to expand the limits of that imagination on behalf of species survival . . . to overcome psychic numbing and . . . , in Martin Buber's words, to "imagine the real." (129–30)

For Lifton, it is only through art that the apocalyptic realities and the global hysteria which characterize history can be rendered bearable, and those few artists who attempt thus to reinscribe history touch the "mythic or formative zone of the psyche" (70). Morrison does this; "imagining the real," she brings us to an awareness of truth beyond "reality" and to an experience beyond "history."

And, as in many other postmodern texts, when history and the concept of reality become so brutal, so horrific and unnatural, the only "natural" element becomes the supernatural. Morrison does not permit us to escape into magic realism; instead, we con- front the fact that evil as it is manifested in history has cosmic reverberations. "Quiet as it's kept," writes Morrison at the open- ing of *The Bluest Eye*, "there were no marigolds in the fall of 1941" (9). And that fact is attributable, not to seeds having been planted too deeply or to the quality of the soil (as Claudia and her sister later rationalize), but to a supernatural reaction to the unnatural fact that "Pecola was having her father's baby" and, even worse, that not a single person in Lorain, Ohio, was able to love or help her. The blight is universal, a cosmically ordained punishment for a community's sin of omission: "the land of the entire country was hostile to marigolds that year. This soil is bad for certain kinds of flowers. Certain seeds it will not nurture, certain fruit it will not bear, and when the land kills of its own volition, we acquiesce and say the victim had no right to live. We are wrong, of course . . . " (160).

The plague of robins that accompanies Sula's return to Medallion in 1937 after an absence of ten years is a similarly unexplainable and supernatural phenomenon, as is the sudden January thaw that follows her death and leads to the deaths of others of the community who, in a mood of mass hysteria, enter the abandoned tunnel—itself a historical artifact and testament to the inevitable failure of the white man's promises—where they are drowned and crushed, entombed. Nature itself, in Morrison's worlds, can manifest evil, an evil deliberate as that of history, construed to punish and chastise:

> They did not believe death was accidental—life might be, but death was deliberate. They did not believe Nature was ever askew—only inconvenient. Plague and drought were as "natural" as springtime. If milk could curdle, God knows robins could fall. The purpose of evil was to survive it and they determined (without ever knowing they had made up their minds to do it) to survive floods, white people, tuberculosis, famine and ignorance. They knew anger well but not despair, and they didn't stone sinners for the same reason they didn't commit suicide—it was beneath them. (*Sula*, 78)

Morrison has said that she writes about "good and evil," but not in "Western terms," that the ways in which a black community responds to evil differ from the ways another community would respond:

> they thought evil had a natural place in the universe; they did not wish to eradicate it. They just wished to protect themselves from it, maybe even to manipulate it, but they never wanted to kill it. They thought evil was just another aspect of life. The ways black people dealt with evil accounted in my mind for how they responded to a lot of other things. It's like a double-

edged sword. . . . It's because they're not terrified by evil, by difference. Evil is not an alien force; it's just a different force. That's the evil I was describing in *Sula*. (Tate 1989, 129)

Evil and its manifestations in the realm of the supernatural are thus an integral part of Morrison's world in which the oxymoron of "magic realism" is perfectly resolved. As Morrison has written about *Song of Solomon*, the novel focuses on "the acceptance of the supernatural and a profound rootedness in the real world at the same time with neither taking precedence over the other. It is indicative of the cosmology, the way in which Black people looked at the world . . . superstition and magic [are] another way of knowing things" (Evans, 339). Toward the end of *Song of Solomon*, Milkman rationalizes, "Jesus! Here he was walking around in the middle of the twentieth century trying to explain what a ghost had done. But why not? he thought. One fact was certain: Pilate did not have a navel. Since that was true, anything could be, and why not ghosts as well?" (298).

Just as she blends distinctions and denies polarities in ideology and identity as well as in language, so Morrison incorporates magic and lore into the realm of reality, revising both in the process. In *Tar Baby*, black folklore as an antidote to "received" history and as an alternative mode of transferring information is invoked by the title and by fictional incorporation of the familiar story of the trickster Rabbit, who is himself tricked by the tar baby from which he cannot separate himself. Son, of course, is the rabbit, and Jadine, product of the white world, is the tar baby (although these roles might conceivably be reversed, depending upon with whom the reader's sympathies lie). But Son is also a kind of frog prince to Jadine's princess, as well as a Black Orpheus to her Eurydice,[1] and, like all characters in love stories, they comprise, finally, an archetype that transcends the story itself. In "The Briar Patch as Modernist Myth: Morrison, Barthes, and Tar Baby As-Is," Craig H. Werner refers to *Tar Baby* as "postmodern metamythology" in which Barthes's theory of myth is linked to the African American folk tradition which "precedes, echoes, and revises it" (151). Samuels and Hudson-Weems state that "Morrison has used folklore and mysticism throughout this novel as a matrix for articulating the interlocking nature of the past and the present as well as the spiritual and the physical worlds" (92). For Son, the blind horsemen of Isle des Chevaliers exist as both history and that revision of history which is legend. His final flight into the swamp to join the horsemen is a flight into a mythic past, into the conjure world, which paradoxically both liberates and annihilates him. Jadine, however, excluded from myth and folklore by her white-world connections, is equally trapped in a present consti-tuted of false realities, and she is surely wrong when she tells Son that "There is nothing any of us can do about the past but make our own lives better" (234).

As Son accepts without question the validity of myth, so that same acceptance of manifestations beyond nature is also intrinsic in *Beloved*: "Not a house in the country ain't packed to its rafters with some dead Negro's grief" (5), says Baby Suggs, who knows that the spirit world is everywhere—in the houses, in the trees, in the rivers, manifested in hellish light or in hands that reach out to caress or to strangle. It is no cause for surprise that Sethe's mur-dered daughter, "Rebuked. Lonely and rebuked" (13), returns "out of blue water" (213) to plague her family and fill the house at 124 Bluestone Road with "baby's venom" (3). The women in that house "understood the source of the outrage as well as they knew the source of light" (4); they accept that "If it's still there waiting, that must mean that nothing ever dies" (36).

Writing itself, for Morrison, is a process of undoing the work of death, of conjuring ghosts, of accounting for "the disremem-bered and unaccounted for" (*Beloved*, 274). It is true that she writes a history and a literature that, as Otten quotes her as say-ing, is "irrevocably, indisputably Black" (1989, 2). She has also told Claudia Tate, "When I view the world, perceive it and write about it, it's the world of black people. It's not that I won't write about white people. I just know that when I'm trying to develop the various themes I write about, the people who best manifest those themes for me are the black people whom I invent" (1989, 118).[2] But Morrison's racial consciousness might well provide a model for all women writers to conceive of history in terms that are different, revolutionary, in a way that, as Cixous writes, "un-thinks the unifying, regulating history that homogenizes and channels forces, herding contradictions into a single battlefield. In woman, personal history blends together with the history of all women, as well as national and world history" (1986, 313).

It seems an understatement to summarize that Morrison reinscribes history just as she inverts both time and Western ontology. In every generation, women writers have struggled to find themselves *within* history, to force or cajole a recognition of their historical existence and their value. Perhaps that has been an error. To re*define* history, as Morrison does, is surely the greater accomplishment—to, as Kristeva says, "set history to rhythm, let us introduce history's rhythm into our discourses, so that we might become the infinitized subject of all histories—be they individual, national, or class histories—which henceforth nothing can totalize" (1980, 203).

4

Rainbows and Brown Sugar: Desire and the Erotic

To Love is to survive paternal meaning.
—Kristeva, *Desire in Language*

Morrison has said that "Love, in the Western notion, is full of possession, distortion, and corruption. It's slaughter without the blood" (Tate 1989, 123). Morrison's novels are always about love and its distortions, and also about slaughter, often *with* the blood; but rarely do they reflect a purely traditional "Western notion" in which desire is repressed, compartmentalized, set apart from the rest of experience, defined, and psychoanalyzed. Outside of the dominant signifying order, writers of the feminine discourse seem to communicate desire differently than men do, and their language to describe pleasure is often untranslatable, indistinguishable from other kinds of experience. For Morrison, the entire world is erotic, and all language is always the expression, the proclamation, of desire.

Eating, for example, is not merely a euphemism for sexual intercourse or an image of sensuality, as occurs in the works of male writers since *Tom Jones*. Rather, in Morrison's texts, food, like everything else in her worlds, is metaphoric, diffusely erotic, expressive of *jouissance*. Meanings radiate, textures permeate, color illuminates—all of which is present, not only in the image, but in the writing itself. The watermelon in *The Bluest Eye* that Cholly Breedlove remembers for the rest of his life appeals not only to the sense of taste; it becomes, in fact, a metaphor for love, an emblem for female sexuality: "Blood red, its planes dull and blunted with sweetness, its edges rigid with juice. Too obvious, almost obscene, in the joy it promised." The seedless, deep red heart, as Cholly places it in his mouth, becomes "The nasty-sweet guts of the earth" (107). This watermelon and the female sexuality it represents have cosmic signification; the great sphere of the fruit, raised high above the head to be split against a rock, becomes "the world," and the man holding it "the strong, black devil . . . blotting out the sun and getting ready to split open the world" (107).

Or: the round, unbearably bright orange that Pilate is eating in *Song of Solomon* the first time Milkman comes to visit signifies a very great deal more than Pilate's own navel-less stomach; Milkman is fascinated by how sensuously she peels the orange and separates the sections, holding each so precisely to her "berry-black" lips: "She held the peelings precisely as they had fallen in her lap, and as she walked up the steps she looked as though she were holding her crotch" (38).[1] If the orange were not sufficient enticement for the dazzled Milkman, who is confronting the female essence for the first time in his life, Pilate also offers that perfect soft-boiled egg: "The yolk I want soft, but not runny. Want it like wet velvet. How come you don't just try one?" (39).

But nowhere in Morrison's work (or perhaps in all of literature) is food more explicitly sexual than is the ice-cream imagery in *Sula*. Preadolescent, "wishbone thin and easy-assed" (45), knowing that "It was too cool for ice cream" (42), Nel and Sula approach "Edna Finch's Mellow House, an ice-cream parlor catering to nice folks—where even children would feel comfortable, you know" (42). The approach to the ice-cream parlor is lined with men, young and old, who "open and close their thighs" as women walk by:

> It was not really Edna Finch's ice cream that made them brave the stretch of those panther eyes. . . . The cream-colored trousers marking with a mere seam the place where the mystery curled. Those smooth vanilla crotches invited them; those lemon-yellow gabardines beckoned to them.
>
> They moved toward the ice-cream parlor like tightrope walkers, as thrilled by the possibility of a slip as by the maintenance of tension and balance. The least sideways glance, the merest toe stub, could pitch them into those creamy haunches spread wide with welcome. Somewhere beneath all of that

daintiness, chambered in all that neatness, lay the thing that clotted their dreams. (43)

Houston A. Baker, Jr., having almost as much fun with this section as Morrison obviously did, comments, "Surely, Edna's mellow confections appear more like the male equivalent of the blues' 'jellyroll' than Baskin-Robbins' twenty-one flavors" (95).[2]

Even in *Beloved*, a much bleaker novel in which joy is the exception, food and sex are metaphorically entwined. Sethe is making biscuits, "fat white circles of dough" (17) lining the pan, as Paul D cups her breasts with his hands for the first time. Also the songs Paul D sings are deeply suggestive: "Little rice, little bean, / No meat in between. / Hard work ain't easy, / Dry bread ain't greasy" (40). And Sethe, who is wise in any number of ways, including the ways of love, knows just what will translate into eroticism:

> On her mind was the supper she wanted to fix for Paul D— something difficult to do, something she would do just so—to launch her newer, stronger life with a tender man. Those litty bitty potatoes browned on all sides, heavy on the pepper; snap beans seasoned with rind; yellow squash sprinkled with vinegar and sugar. Maybe corn cut from the cob and fried with green onions and butter. Raised bread, even. (99–100)

Whether or not Sethe ever actually cooks this dinner ("soul food" indeed) is left to the reader's imagination, for just reciting the menu to Paul D is sufficiently appetizing to drive them both upstairs to bed. Years earlier, Sethe remembers, she and Halle had consummated their marriage in the cornfields of Sweet Home, imagining they had privacy, while in reality the other men, denied expression of their own sexuality, sat, "erect as dogs," watching "corn stalks dance at noon." The following feast on the corn plucked from the broken stalks becomes a signification for virgin sex:

> The pulling down of the tight sheath, the ripping sound always convinced her it hurt.
> As soon as one strip of husk was down, the rest obeyed and the ear yielded up to him its shy rows, exposed at last. How loose the silk. How quick the jailed-up flavor ran free.
> No matter what all your teeth and wet fingers anticipated,

there was no accounting for the way that simple joy could
shake you.
　　How loose the silk. How fine and loose and free. (27)

　　But food, even candy, is not always so erotic, linked though
it inevitably is with sexuality and, most frequently, with humor.
In *Tar Baby*, the "Valerians," manufactured by Valerian Street's
father and named for Valerian, are "red and white gumdrops in a
red and white box (mint-flavored, the white ones; strawberry-
flavored, the red)." The fake flavors and the sickeningly sweet Val-
entine sentiments they symbolize are metaphors for Valerian's
own questionable masculinity and, presumably, for that of all
white men. Black children will not buy them because the candies
are "faggoty. . . . Can you see a kid sitting on a curb tossing those
fairy candies in his mouth? . . . Give us something with nuts, why
don't you? . . . Nobody can make a dollar selling faggot candy to
jigs" (42–43). Significantly, Valerian's wife is also "all red and
white, like the Valerians" (43). Son, on the other hand, is called
"the chocolate eater," and the racial reference is obvious.

　　Candy in *The Bluest Eye*, particularly the Mary Janes that Pecola sacrifices so much of her pride to buy, becomes an emblem
of shame in its association with white privilege and of envy for
the blue eyes of the little blonde girl depicted on the package. To
eat the candy, however, is also orgasmic, sexual, an act of possession, even of violence; surely Pecola is practicing some secular
communion, or perhaps she enacts a primitive rite of passage, a
cannibal feast, as she gorges herself on the body of the enemy in
order to assume its power: "To eat the candy is somehow to eat
the eyes, eat Mary Jane. Love Mary Jane. Be Mary Jane. Three
pennies had bought her nine lovely orgasms with Mary Jane.
Lovely Mary Jane, for whom a candy is named" (43).

　　Even more sombre is the image of candy in *Song of Solomon*;
Guitar grows ill even at the smell of sweets, which make him
"think of dead people. And white people. And I start to puke"
(61). But it is not only the memory of sweet white divinity given
by the white boss to Guitar in compensation for the death of his
father that makes him sick, but the recollection of his mother's
sweet acquiescence, her utter victimization; and his fury is directed at her and at all women who are similarly accessible. The
peppermint stick his mother buys for him on the day of his
father's funeral is surely a surrogate penis, but one that only
serves to emphasize his own impotence to protect his mother, or

any woman; therefore, he discards the candy as he discards the women: "he could not eat it or throw it away, until finally, in the outhouse, he let it fall into the earth's stinking hole" (227). As an adult, Guitar is incapable of relationships with women, preferring the male camaraderie of the Seven Days and his vaguely homoerotic friendship with Milkman, "My man. . . . My main man" (341).

Similarly, Milkman associates the "faintly sweet" taste of his mother's milk with both shame and impotence, recalling the darkened and secret room in which she daily reenacted the ritual of a grotesque and carnivalesque *pietà*, the perversity with which she nursed him until his feet reached the floor, the sexuality with which she unbuttoned her blouse, closed her eyes, and smiled (13). Milkman shares more than a little in Macon Dead's opinion of his son's nickname: "It sounded dirty, intimate, and hot" (15). In fact, all food prepared by the mother in this family is unacceptable: "She did not try to make her meals nauseating; she simply didn't know how not to" (11). Interestingly, for this particular meal, Ruth substitutes a rennet dessert for the impossibly difficult sunshine cake. It cannot be surprising, then, given the food symbolism in this novel and the association of the mother and all women, except Pilate, with a sensation of nausea, that Milkman has such difficulty committing himself to sexual relationships with women.

Milk and the image of motherhood are most particularly associated with male impotence in *Beloved*, as Halle watches helplessly from the loft above while Schoolteacher's nephews violate Sethe so brutally by taking her milk. Halle's response to his inability to protect his wife from such perversity, such outrageous violence, is to go mad, to smear butter and clabber over his own face almost in imitation of the act he has witnessed, to disintegrate completely. Up to this point, Halle has been a noble figure, a good husband and son, the best of the Sweet Home men, all of whom are respectful to each other and to Sethe. But here the outrage is unbearable, and he loses his manhood with his sanity. Finally, he is less strong than Sethe, who is condemned to her sanity by the necessity to survive for her children's sake: "Other people went crazy, why couldn't she? . . . And how sweet that would have been: the two of them back by the milk shed, squatting by the churn, smashing cold, lumpy butter into their faces with not a care in the world" (70).

A similar event to that Halle cannot endure, the inability to protect the woman for whom one perceives responsibility, occurs also in *The Bluest Eye*. The reader's sympathy for Cholly Breedlove, despite his later unforgivable action of raping his daughter, is assured by that scene in which, having been discovered by white hunters just as he is about to make love for the first time in his life, he is unable to protect either himself or Darlene from the obscenities that follow. Not milk, but the taste of unripe muscadine grapes, their bloodlike stains covering Darlene's white dress, are associated with sex and its failure in this instance, and "the sweet taste of muscadine" turns to "rotten fetid bile" (117), as Cholly transfers his hatred for the hunters into hatred for Darlene, holding her responsible for his impotence. As Davis explains in "Self, Society, and Myth in Toni Morrison's Fiction":

> The desire to "protect" her was the desire to create himself as her protector. All he can do to restore his selfhood is to deny hers further. In the recurring scene of black male resentment at black women's submission to oppression (the soldiers' stony stares at Helene and the conductor, Guitar's hatred of his mother's smile and of Pilate's "Aunt Jemima act"), Morrison shows the displacement of male humiliation onto the only person left that a black man can "own"—the black woman. . . . The black woman—doubly Other—is the perfect scapegoat. (330)

Male impotence and images of castration, whether created by female submission or female power, are certainly problematic for a great many readers and critics of Morrison's work as well as that of other black American women writers. Richard K. Barksdale, one example among many, links Morrison with Alice Walker and Paule Marshall, holding all guilty of producing "within the context of the feminist movement a fictional whirlwind of protest over what history has wrought": "Their message is clear and direct: because of the wanton abuse of his assumed superior sexual status, the black male of the twentieth century has become a psychological and economic disaster who should be promptly castrated and cast aside on history's junkpile. And the prototypical male castaway can be found in abundant numbers on the pages of their fiction" (407). While a full discussion of this controversy is beyond the scope and interest of this study,[3] one must agree that a great many of Morrison's male characters are, in fact, psychological and economic disasters, symbolically castrated and rendered infantile and ineffectual. In her novels, however, such depictions are most often justified by historical conditions (see Chapter 3) and explicable by at least the partial responsibility of her female characters, most obviously those archaic and phallic mothers, those strong and dominant food-givers and man-eaters who bond together in twos and threes, and who dictate the terms of their own metafictions. That Morrison herself trembles before their power should be obvious from discussions in previous chapters.

Least complex because least developed of these figures are the three prostitutes in *The Bluest Eye*. So castrating are these women that it is a wonder they have customers at all, for

> these women hated men, all men, without shame, apology, or discrimination. They abused their visitors with a scorn grown mechanical from use. Black men, white men, Puerto Ricans, Mexicans, Jews, Poles, whatever—all were inadequate and weak, all came under their jaundiced eyes and were the recipients of their disinterested wrath. They took delight in cheating them. On one occasion the town well knew, they lured a Jew up the stairs, pounced on him, all three, held him up by the heels, shook everything out of his pants pockets, and threw him out of the window. (47–48)

This is broad, even slapstick comedy, but the three whores are also a prototype for their more sinister sisters in later novels, in which Morrison is not laughing but extending a cautionary example, a warning to women readers and feminist critics that, if women participate in the castration of men, whether through love or malice (both and either of which is effective toward this end), they will end up with no men at all, only children.

As almost every critic of *Sula* has noted, most males in this novel are infantilized, even by their very names: BoyBoy, Tar Baby, Sweet Plum, Chicken Little. And, they behave accordingly: abandoning families, going insane, becoming alcoholic or drug-addicted. Only the women in this novel have "real" names, and they are the agents of power, even of castration—at least symbolically. Sula and Nel are formidable adversaries of men even when they are preadolescent. Certainly the threat is of castration in that incident in which Sula and Nel, coming home from school, are bullied by a group of white boys. In parody of a circumcision rite, Sula takes a knife and cuts off the tip of her own finger: "If I can do that to myself, what you suppose I'll do to you?" (47). Even white boys understand how dangerous she is: "The shifting dirt was the only way Nel knew that they were moving away" (47).

More threatening is the following series of events, which takes place shortly after the ice-cream parlor episode. It is the summer, "limp with the weight of blossomed things" and of "The beautiful, beautiful boys who dotted the landscape like jewels. . . . Even their footprints left a smell of smoke behind" (48). Nature itself and the corresponding blossoming maturity of Nel and Sula seem to demand some ritual, what Baker terms a "three-fold enactment of Phallic rites" (97). But this might also be a defloration ritual, like those performed in connection with some historical matriarchal cultures. Nel and Sula sit beside a river, playing with two thick twigs which they have "undressed," "stripped to a smooth, creamy innocence" (49–50):

> But soon [Nel] grew impatient and poked her twig rhythmically and intensely into the earth, making a small neat hole that grew deeper and wider with the least manipulation of her twig. Sula copied her, and soon each had a hole the size of a cup. Nel began a more strenuous digging and, rising to her knees, was careful to scoop out the dirt as she made her hole deeper. Together they worked until the two holes were one and the same. When the depression was the size of a small dishpan, Nel's twig broke. With a gesture of disgust she threw the pieces into the hole they had made. Sula threw hers in too. Nel saw a bottle cap and tossed it in as well. Each then looked around for more debris to throw into the hole: paper, bits of glass, butts of cigarettes, until all the small defiling things they could find were collected there. Carefully they replaced the soil and covered the entire grave with uprooted grass.
> Neither one had spoken a word. (50)

Immediately following these ceremonies and this significant silence (see Chapter 1 for a discussion of similar symbolic silences) is the ritualized sacrifice of the male-child; Chicken Little happens by, innocently picking his nose: "You scared we gone take your bugger away?" Sula teases. His name, according to Baker, is "Morrison's own mocking designation of the Phallus, in all of its mystery, as a false harbinger of apocalypse" (98). The apocalypse, however, is Chicken Little's own; Sula swings him out over the water—and lets go.

The butterflies that fly among the flowers on Chicken Little's grave presage the butterflies Ajax brings as courtship offering to Sula, just as the stick ceremony has presaged the sexual relationships of both Nel and Sula. While Nel's adolescent dreams of "lying on a flowered bed, tangled in her own hair, waiting for some fiery prince" (44) prefigure her passivity in her marriage to Jude, Sula's dreams indicate the active sexual power she will assume as she gallops "through her own mind on a gray-and-white horse tasting sugar and smelling roses in full view of a someone who shared both the taste and the speed" (44).

"It was manlove that Eva bequeathed to her daughters" (35), Morrison's narrator tells us, and like Hannah, who required "some touching every day" (38), Sula enjoys sex for its own sake and for the reflection of her own power that it provides:

> During the lovemaking she found and needed to find the cutting edge. When she left off cooperating with her body and began to assert herself in the act, particles of strength gathered in her like steel shavings drawn to a spacious magnetic center, forming a tight cluster that nothing, it seemed, could break. And there was utmost irony and outrage in lying under someone in a position of surrender, feeling her own abiding strength and limitless power. But the cluster did break, fall apart, and in her panic to hold it together she leaped from the edge into soundlessness and went down howling, howling in a stinging awareness of the endings of things, an eye of sorrow in the midst of all that hurricane rage of joy. (106)

Thus does Morrison give a voice to female desire by providing what is possibly the best description in American literature of the feminine orgasm; it is *jouissance*, in fact—a transcendent experience that reclaims the female body from the male inscription—but it is also an expression of pain, a complex howl of sorrow that is both birth and death, political and even cosmic in its implications.

With Ajax, who loves the female power in Sula as he has loved it in his own mother, Sula assumes the upper position, swaying "like a Georgia pine on its knees, high above the slipping, falling smile, high above the golden eyes," drifting toward "the high silence of orgasm. . . . He swallowed her mouth just as her thighs had swallowed his genitals, and the house was very, very quiet" (112–13). Baker writes that this is a rewriting, perhaps even a retraction, of the phallic ceremony of childhood: "The swallowing of the actual penis, rather than the burial of the Phallus, might produce a resounding quiet and a genuine Peace" (102). But perhaps Sula's aims are less redemptive than Baker indicates, for surely there is ambiguity, if not actual violence, in her fantasy that accompanies the sexual act: "If I take a chamois and rub real hard on the bone, right on the ledge of your cheek bone, some of the black will disappear. . . . And if I take a nail file or even Eva's old paring knife—that will do—and scrape away at the gold. . . . Then I can take a chisel and small tap hammer . . . " (112). According to Patricia Yaeger, similar literary renditions of the "female sublime" constitute a "liberating structure of female violence and aggression" (1989, 209).

Baker also argues that this sexual relationship between Sula and Ajax redeems the heterosexuality which suffers as an ideal so frequently in Morrison's novels and serves to invalidate Barbara Smith's argument in "Toward a Black Feminist Criticism" for *Sula* as a lesbian novel.[4] Morrison herself has unequivocally stated that "there is no homosexuality in *Sula*" (Tate 1989, 118). But Smith is certainly correct in her appraisal of the consistent failure of heterosexual relationships in Morrison's fiction. Even Ajax, that phenomenal lover, cannot cope with Sula's possessive demands, and he leaves for a Dayton air show. Sula, like Nel, like Eva and Hannah, is finally abandoned. For Morrison, *jouissance* always depends upon escape from patriarchally sanctified sexuality, upon freedom from romantic ideals like love and possession. Sula's temporary surrender of her own life-giving eroticism in her attempt to possess Ajax, her lapse into domesticity signified by the green hair ribbon and the sparkling bathroom, not only alienate Ajax but represent her own death knell, her descent into a sleep of "cobalt blue" where "she tasted the acridness of gold, left the chill of alabaster and smelled the dark, sweet stench of loam" (118).

Ajax, like so many of Morrison's men, is effectively though symbolically castrated, not by Sula, despite her nail file and knives fantasy, but by his own mother, "an evil conjure woman, blessed with seven adoring children whose joy it was to bring her the plants, hair, underclothing, fingernail parings, white hens, blood, camphor, pictures, kerosene, and footstep dust that she needed. . . . She knew about weather, omens, the living, the dead, dreams and all illnesses" (109). Sula herself is witchlike by this point in the novel; but she cannot replace the mother, although a surrogate for his mother is what Ajax really wants; he brings Sula a bottle of milk on his first visit, which he drinks himself. But Sula has not named him, and, in fact, has incorrectly called him Ajax when his name was Albert Jacks: "so how could he help but leave me since he was making love to a woman who didn't even know his name" (117).

To name is to have power over the individual named, as was discussed in Chapter 2, and the namer in *Sula* is Eva, whose power is symbolic of her function as the phallic mother to destroy as well as to create life. There is no question that she loves her children; she has sacrificed even her leg (which is no castration symbol in this case) to provide for them; to relieve the baby Plum's life-threatening constipation, as Eva recites ritualistically and repeatedly, she has taken a lump of lard and "shoved the last bit of food she had in the world (besides three beets) up his ass" (29). But Plum returns from war to his mother's house a drug addict, helpless as an infant again. She murders him, burns him alive in his bed, because he "wanted to crawl back in my womb:"

> I ain't got the room no more even if he could do it. There wasn't space for him in my womb. And he was crawlin' back. Being helpless and thinking baby thoughts and dreaming baby dreams and messing up his pants again and smiling all the time. I had room enough in my heart, but not in my womb, got no more. I birthed him once. I couldn't do it again. He was growed, a big old thing. Godhavemercy, I couldn't birth him twice . . . so I just thought of a way he could die like a man not all crunched up inside my womb, but like a man. . . . But I held him close first. Real close. Sweet Plum. My baby boy. (62)

As Eva pours the kerosene over her son, before she lights the match, he feels the sensation of "an eagle pouring a wet lightness over him. Some kind of baptism, some kind of blessing" (40). The fire Eva lights is as paradoxical as her love; it purifies as it destroys. As Clément and Cixous define the "sorceress" who haunts our dreams, "She is innocent, mad, full of badly remembered memories, guilty of unknown wrongs; she is the seductress, the heiress of all generic Eves" (6).

Also, as Rubenstein has suggested in *Boundaries of the Self: Gender, Culture, Fiction*, Morrison's novels are replete with images of incest, desired or enacted. Like that of Ajax, Plum's desire to return to the mother is unconscious, but, more perversely, Eva is perfectly aware of her own desire to permit that return:

> I'd be laying here at night and he be downstairs in that room, but when I closed my eyes I'd see him . . . six feet tall smilin' and crawlin' up the stairs quietlike so I wouldn't hear and open-ing the door soft so I wouldn't hear and he'd be creepin' to the bed trying to spread my legs. . . . One night it wouldn't be no dream. It'd be true and I would have done it, would have let him. . . . (62)

The return to the mother, erotic as this return always is in all of Morrison's novels, is also always associated with castration, death, oblivion, but also—paradoxically—with enlightenment, revelation, transcendence. For the women assembled at Chicken Little's funeral, all the dead sons become "Sweet Jesus" himself, who is both "son and lover in whose downy face they could see the sugar-and-butter sandwiches and feel the oldest and most dev-astating pain there is: not the pain of childhood, but the remem-brance of it" (56). In *Desire in Language*, Kristeva refers to a "non-Oedipal incest" that "opens the eyes of a subject who is nourished by the mother . . . neither animal, god, nor man, he is Dionysus, born a second time for having had the mother" (192). The artist of a culture, says Kristeva, is one who seeks maternal *jouissance*, who is a "servant to the maternal phallus" (246).

"Artist" or not, Milkman in *Song of Solomon* also seeks the maternal phallus, not in his own ineffectual and powerless mother, but in his aunt, Pilate, who, as discussed earlier, is a mother sur-rogate and as powerful as Eva or any other of Morrison's archaic mothers. Pilate is also a seductress in her offering of food and her telling of tales, and Milkman is unconsciously drawn to her in ways that are often sexual. In Shalimar, Milkman considers the beautiful women he sees all around him, and he is reminded of Pilate: "They sat on porches, and walked in the road swaying their hips under cotton dresses, bare-legged, their unstraightened hair braided or pulled straight back into a ball. He wanted one of them bad. To curl up in a cot in that one's arms, or that one, or that. That's the way Pilate must have looked as a girl, looked even now . . . " (266). Both Pilate and Circe represent for Milkman the forbidden part of himself, that zone of the erotic that subverts reason and patriarchal inscriptions; he is quite literally bewitched by them:

> He had had dreams as a child, dreams every child had, of the witch who chased him down dark alleys, between lawn trees, and finally into rooms from which he could not escape. Witches in black dresses and red underskirts; witches with pink eyes and green lips, tiny witches, long rangy witches, frowning witches, smiling witches, screaming witches and laughing witches, witches that flew, witches that ran, and some that merely glided on the ground . . . but he knew that always, always at the very instant of the pounce or the gummy embrace he would wake with a scream and an erection. Now he had only the erection. (241–42)

Pilate is an Eve figure, as was mentioned earlier, but she is also the snake of Macon Dead's imagination (54), and the crawling, flying witch of Milkman's dreams. Finally, she is the "Sugargirl" of Milkman's death song on the last page: "There must be another one like you. . . . There's got to be at least one more woman like you" (340).

Just as Hagar cannot hope to compete with Pilate for Milkman's affection or Sula to replace Ajax's powerful mother, so Jadine in *Tar Baby* cannot succeed in her attempts to rescue Son from the "diaspora mothers," the ancestor figures, the witches with the magic breasts: "She thought she was rescuing him from the night women who wanted him for themselves, wanted him feeling superior in a cradle, deferring to him. . . . Mama-spoiled black man, will you mature with me? Culture-bearing black woman, whose culture are you bearing?" (231–32). But Son, as his name indicates, has always belonged to the mothers and the night women, to the wild zone.

Son's very inaccessibility and his wildness are what attract Jadine in the first place, along with his potential for violence, which fits perfectly into her unconscious rape fantasies. His skin is very black in contrast to her diluted coloring, and he wears his hair in dreadlocks: "his hair looked overpowering—physically overpowering, like bundles of long whips or lashes that could grab her and beat her to jelly. And would. Wild, aggressive, vicious hair that needed to be put in jail. Uncivilized, reform-school hair. Mau Mau, Attica, chain-gang hair" (97). Part of Jadine's fascination is a perversion of racial stereotypes, her own aspiration to "whiteness" depending on a rejection of what she defines in herself as "black" and what she interprets as animal sexuality: "Like an animal. Treating her like another animal and both of them must have looked just like it in that room. One dog sniffing at the hindquarters of another" (105–6). Jadine revels in such fantasies, debased not so much by Son as by her own imagination. Her "animal" self is in reality masturbatorially manifested by the baby sealskin coat, gift of a white male admirer, on which she lies naked and "spread-eagled . . . nestling herself into it. It made her tremble. She opened her lips and licked the fur" (96). Jadine's perversity is no less than that of Margaret Street, who is also titillated by the potential violence Son represents in her neurotic white woman's fantasy of the black rapist who has hidden himself in her closet, "Actually in her things. Probably jerking off. Black sperm was sticking in clots to her French jeans or down in the toe of her Anne Klein shoes. Didn't men sometimes jerk off in women's shoes?" (73).

And there is much basis in such fantasies, for Son's sexual philosophy includes the viability of violence and the conviction of male superiority, as he indicates in his first conversation with Valerian in the greenhouse: women, he says, are like plants; "you have to jack them up every once in a while. Make em act nice, like they're supposed to" (127). Son has murdered one wife, and he does beat Jadine, for all of which the night women forgive him, although, one hopes, Morrison does not. Even though Son is metaphorically the male soldier ant of Jadine's jungle fantasy, fertilizing the queen ant and doing "the single thing he was born for," which the queen remembers until the fortieth generation, and even though he is "the man who fucked like a star" (250–51)—"Star throbs. Over and over and over. Like this. Stars just throb and throb and throb and sometimes, when they can't throb anymore, when they can't hold it anymore, they fall out of the sky" (184)—his destiny is finally the mother space of the swamp, the reentry into the womb. "Small boy," Thérèse addresses him, as she directs him into oblivion.

Many women in Morrison's fictions, and most particularly the mother-women, are often servile and indulgent, if only with their sons, and thus they are guilty of destroying the very sons about whom they are so passionate, rendering them into chronic infancy, usurping their masculinity, and effectively ensuring that they are unfit for adult sexual relationships with other women. But Morrison's men, too, are often responsible for their own condition; they have surrendered masculinity deliberately and of their own free will, preferring the role of pampered infant. Milkman, for example, has accepted the homage and deference of women whom he has, in turn, mistreated all his life, so locked is he in the prison of his male ego. His very walk is characterized, not by a limp as he imagines, but by a strut. He himself is so like the male peacock with the jeweled tail that he and Guitar admire, and he so richly deserves his sisters' scorn:

> Our girlhood was spent like a found nickel on you. When you slept, we were quiet; when you were hungry, we cooked; when you wanted to play, we entertained you; and when you got grown enough to know the difference between a woman and a two-toned Ford, everything in this house stopped for you. You have yet to wash your underwear, spread a bed, wipe the ring from your tub, or move a fleck of your dirt from one place to another. . . . You are a sad, pitiful, stupid, selfish, hateful man. I hope your little hog's gut stands you in good stead, and that you take good care of it, because you don't have anything else . . . you have pissed your last in this house. (216–18)

Although there is some regeneration for Milkman by the end of the novel in his recognition that "From the beginning, his mother and Pilate had fought for his life, and he had never so much as made either of them a cup of tea" (335), and in his compensatory action of repaying Sweet's kindnesses by rubbing her back and cleaning her tub, it is all ironically too late and too little.

Nel's husband, Jude, in *Sula* is similarly and deservingly castigated by Sula, who answers his plea for feminine sympathy and comfort with the statement that "everything in the world loves you. . . . And if that ain't enough, you love yourselves. Nothing in this world loves a black man more than another black man" (89). Morrison herself is surely outraged at male behavior, and the feminist reader cheers her on, feels vindicated and grateful. And we are grateful, too, when she finally redeems the male sex and provides us with the closest thing to a "fiery prince" that she can conjure.

One of the few male characters in Morrison's novels who survives as a hero, who is able to withstand maternal aggression at least for a time, and who preserves his life, his manhood, and his dignity, is Paul D in *Beloved*. Perhaps because his suffering under slavery has been equal to Sethe's, or perhaps because he has retained the ancient African worship for womanhood in general as well as for the Great Mother, Paul D has "the thing in him, the blessedness, that has made him the kind of man who can walk in a house and make the women cry. Because with him, in his presence, they could. Cry and tell him things they only told each other" (272). He is "a singing man," "a tender man," and he understands the female language:

> Trust and rememory, yes, the way she believed it could be when he cradled her before the cooking stove. The weight and angle of him; the true-to-life beard hair on him; arched back, educated hands. His waiting eyes and awful human power. The mind of him that knew her own. Her story was bearable because it was his as well—to tell, to refine and tell again. The things that neither knew about the other—the things neither had word-shapes for—well, it would come in time. . . . (99)

As I discussed in Chapter 1, the body and the word become synonymous, and both are erotic; Paul D "wants to put his story next to hers" (273). Or perhaps the eroticism so inherent in this relationship comes from the context of history itself, the continuing presence of danger or death, the necessity to seize the erotic moment from a hostile world, the need to affirm a life that is not a gift but that is stolen from history. Paul D meets Sethe on the street one winter afternoon, and they share such a moment:

> She let her head touch his chest, and since the moment was valuable to both of them, they stopped and stood that way— not breathing, not even caring if a passerby passed them by. The winter light was low. Sethe closed her eyes. Paul D looked at the black trees lining the roadside, their defending arms raised against attack. Softly, suddenly, it began to snow, like a present come down from the sky. Sethe opened her eyes to it and said, "Mercy." And it seemed to Paul D that it was—a little mercy—something given to them on purpose to mark what they were feeling so they would remember it later on when they needed to.
>
> Down came the dry flakes, fat enough and heavy enough to crash like nickels on stone. It always surprised him, how quiet it was. Not like rain, but like a secret. (129)

But even the love of Paul D cannot totally compensate for the reality of the atrocities that are history; no purely edenic return is possible in Morrison's world. The reader cannot help but interpret Paul D's almost incestuous sexual surrender to Beloved's supernatural powers as a betrayal. Nor can he, being merely human, easily confront the face of female murder; even he wavers before that which Sethe represents—the phallic mother, the Medusa.

However, like Paul D and like Milkman and Son, all of Morrison's male characters are helpless with desire for the Great Mother—terrifying though she always is, representing as she always does the violation of the law of the father. The desire for the mother is itself a form of incest, and incest in all its guises, according to Freud, is an expression of the human desire for disorder, counterorder. And this is true for Morrison as well, although she makes no moral judgments about the nature of disorder, recognizing it as dangerous but also as a valid aspect of human experience. Those of Morrison's characters who have not encountered their own jungles, never been enmeshed within the preoedipal bond, never explored the foreign territory of their own sexuality, are condemned to innocence in which they suffer the extreme deprivation of their humanity.[5]

There are also those characters, however, who lose humanity through an excess of freedom, whose drive to disorder is so unfettered that it becomes destructive to self as well as to others. Cholly Breedlove in *The Bluest Eye* is one such character, guilty of what Morrison terms "illicit, traumatic, incomprehensible sex coming to its dreaded fruition" (1990, 219), which is the rape of his daughter. But even this dreadful event, within Morrison's ethical system, punished as it is with disgrace and death, is nonetheless at least partially understandable, a "hatred mixed with tenderness" (129). As Morrison has explained in an interview, "I want you to *look* at him and see his love for his daughter and his powerlessness to help her pain. By that time his embrace, the rape, is all the gift he has left" (Tate 1989, 125).

For Morrison, however, extreme repression is even more destructive than unfettered freedom. Cholly's wife, Pauline, has lost her sexual self in her rage for order and her fascination with the cleanliness (sterility) of the white woman's kitchen, in which she could "arrange things, clean things, line things up in neat rows" (101). Religion replaces sexuality as a far more destructive drive, entailing an idea, not of morality, but of revenge: "Mrs. Breedlove was not interested in Christ the Redeemer, but rather Christ the Judge" (37). And her battles with Cholly involving both psychological abuse and physical violence are of epic scope; these take place, not in order for her to save his soul or he hers, for each needs the excesses of the other to exist, but to forget that there was once another kind of existence, another place in which sex was erotic rather than merely violent and where rainbows could be both seen and felt: "those little bits of color floating up into me—deep in me. That streak of green from the june-bug light, the purple from the berries trickling along my thighs. . . . Then I feel like I'm laughing between my legs, and the laughing gets all mixed up with the colors, and I'm afraid I'll come, and afraid I won't. But I know I will. And I do. And it be rainbow all inside . . . " (103–4).

Pauline's life is ugly and violent, but it is some compensation that she has such memories, the preservation of which is surely her intention when she refuses her white woman employer's well-meaning but culturally obtuse advice to leave Cholly, to deny her own sexual reality. Pauline is thus fortunate in comparison to that amorphous group of "sugar-brown Mobile girls" who have lost their sugar, who spend their lives fighting "the dreadful funkiness of passion," and who build their nests, "stick by stick" (68–69), even to the destruction of husbands and sons. One such woman who does not "sweat in her armpits nor between her thighs" (70) is Geraldine, who never kisses her baby boy and thus turns him into the monster who so tortures Pecola with his mother's only erotic object, that pathetic remnant of lost witchcraft and female power, her cat:

> The cat will settle quietly on the windowsill and caress her with his eyes. She can hold him in her arms, letting his back paws struggle for footing on her breast and his forepaws cling to her shoulder. She can rub the smooth fur and feel the unresisting flesh underneath. . . . When she stands cooking at the table, he will circle about her shanks, and the trill of his fur spirals up her legs to her thighs, to make her fingers tremble a little in the pie dough. (70)

Nel of *Sula* has no comparable familiar, but she is more than a bit like Geraldine, particularly after she is married to Jude and thus estranged from the wild side of herself, which is Sula. Nel's

adolescent dreams of passive sexuality are manifest in her indul-
gence of a husband who only seeks another mother; his desire is
for a woman who will sympathize with the pain he suffers at the
hands of the white man, who will be the "the hem—the tuck and
fold that hid his raveling edges; a someone sweet, industrious and
loyal to shore him up. . . . Without that someone he was a waiter
hanging around a kitchen like a woman. With her he was head of
a household pinned to an unsatisfactory job out of necessity. The
two of them together would make one Jude" (71). In her willing
assumption of the role Jude requires, Nel effectively depletes his
integrity and his masculinity along with her own female power,
thereby assuring his eventual desertion of her, her own sexual
deprivation, and her own misery. Ajax is right about some
women: "all they want, man, is they own misery. Ax em to die for
you and they yours for life" (71).

Guitar, himself psychologically fit only for celibacy in the
priesthood of the Seven Days, says to Hagar in *Song of Solomon*:
"You're turning over your whole life to him. Your whole life, girl.
And if it means so little to you that you can just give it away, hand
it to him, then why should it mean any more to him? . . . Pretty
little black-skinned woman. Who wanted to kill for love, die for
love" (310). Dying for love, in fact, is a part of African American
folklore, the subject of music and stories, and Hagar is no aber-
ration in this respect: "The lengths to which lost love drove men
and women never surprised them. They had seen women pull
their dresses over their heads and howl like dogs for lost love"
(128). But, in the case of Hagar, there is truly something "askew,"
as even Ruth Foster can detect: not a "wilderness where there was
system, or the logic of lions, trees, toads, and birds, but wild wilderness where there was none" (138).

Perhaps Hagar's "wilderness" comes from her life experience
in the mother space, the preoedipal condition of Pilate's house,
where she is the pampered daughter, the only one with sheets on
her bed, the loved and spoiled darling. Pilate introduces her to
Milkman as "your brother" (43), and the forbidden, incestuous
nature of their long relationship is characterized by the image of
wilderness, violence, and ultimately by Milkman's reenactment of
his great grandfather's flight from responsibility and Hagar's
death from sorrow, which imitates Ryna's destruction. "My baby
girl," Pilate mourns at Hagar's funeral, and her words are tossed
"like stones into a silent canyon" (323), that same canyon that is

Ryna's Gulch in which the cries of abandoned women echo throughout the centuries.

But dying for love, Morrison implies, is better than dying for the lack of it, and, particularly in *Song of Solomon*, there are a great many women who do just that. Ruth Foster, for example, has a husband named "Dead," which indicates more than his personality, for he has punished her for years by denying her (although not thereby himself as well, it is hinted) sexual gratification. In Morrison's terms, Ruth is like "a lighthouse keeper," "a prisoner automatically searching out the sun" (11), and her perversions—nursing her half-grown son and, according to her husband's account, sucking the fingers of her dead father—shrink in comparison to that most perverse behavior of Macon Dead's. And Macon has terrorized his daughters as well, seeking to doom them to perpetual virginity, the velvet rose petals they spend their time in manufacturing being emblematic of their enforced and artificial condition. Lena tells Milkman about the significance of making the roses: "I loved to do it. It kept me . . . quiet. That's why they make those people in the asylum weave baskets and make rag rugs. It keeps them quiet. If they didn't have the baskets they might find out what's really wrong and . . . do something. Something terrible" (215). Rather than relive her mother's madness, Corinthians, Milkman's other sister, will in fact do "something terrible," which is to prostrate herself on the hood of Porter's old car, begging for his love, his sex, anything but the roses: "This is for you, girl. Oh, yes. This is for you" (201).[6]

Deprivation of sexual love is catastrophic for almost all characters in Morrison's novels, and perversity, even madness and brutality, is more likely to coincide with sexual abstinence than with sexual excess. Chastity is the key to Soaphead Church's perverse love for "clean little girls" in *The Bluest Eye*, and his confusion of lovemaking with "communion and the Holy Grail" loses him his wife who "had not lived by the sea all those years, listened to the wharfman's songs all that time, to spend her life in the soundless cave of Elihue's mind" (134). Prudently, Velma refuses to play the role of Beatrice, refuses to be robbed of her own sexuality and subsumed into the stereotype of a diseased male fantasy that cannot cope with life or with the living woman.

Male discomfort with and denial of female sexuality is a pattern in Morrison's fiction, just as it is in Cixous's ironically hu-

morous analyses: "Conquering her, they've made haste to depart
from her borders, to get out of sight, out of body. . . . One can
understand how man, confusing himself with his penis and rush-
ing in for the attack, might feel resentment and fear of being
'taken' by the woman, of being lost in her, absorbed or alone"
(310). Sexual deprivation, apparently, is the price for female
power, but also paradoxically, for the surrender of power. For Nel
in *Sula*, the loss of, not Jude himself, but Jude's sexuality is so
debilitating that death seems preferable:

> And what am I supposed to do with these old thighs now, just
> walk up and down these rooms? What good are they, Jesus?
> They will never give me the peace I need to get from sunup to
> sundown. . . . O Jesus, I could be a mule or plow the furrows
> with my hands if need be or hold these rickety walls up with
> my back if need be if I knew that somewhere in this world in
> the pocket of some night I could open my legs to some cowboy
> lean hips but you are trying to tell me no and O my sweet Jesus
> what kind of cross is that? (95–96)

Sexual deprivation, too, is the source of Margaret's rape fantasies
about Son in *Tar Baby*, but even more significantly, it is the ostensible reason behind her abuse of her own son as well as the conscious process of self-annihilation that occupies her life. The "dark
continent" of feminine sensibility and eroticism, according to Cixous and Clément, is in reality "neither dark nor unexplorable"
(68), at least not for women, and most particularly not for
Morrison.

"To *love*," says Kristeva in *Desire in Language*, "is to survive
paternal meaning" (150). But sex and even love are finally not
separable from paternal meaning; they do not save the world or
even the individual in Morrison's fictions, where the edenic return
remains firmly in the realm of the imagination rather than in the
area of possibility. Morrison does not offer redemption through
her portrayal of sexuality but only reminders: "Not love, but a
willingness to love" (*Song of Solomon*, 226).

And yet always in Morrison's texts there *is* a possible kind of
redemption through that which is erotic: it lies in her language,
resonates in her imagery, provides meaning and texture to structure. Another kind of *jouissance* apparently exists in the pleasures

of the writerly text. At the close of Chapter 1 it was suggested that Morrison writes the female body, that her texts imitate and recreate the feminine orgasm, that they constitute what Cixous calls "the flesh of language," the "feminine" style, "the savage tongue" (1981, 52). Morrison's language itself is erotic, an erogenous zone, so full of color and rainbows and summer smoke: "Jesus, there were some beautiful boys in 1921. . . . The sun heated them and the moon slid down their backs. God, the world was *full* of beautiful boys in 1921" (*Sula*, 140). Finally, her rendering of the erotic and the feminine is so euphoric and so life-giving that we hardly recognize the failure of love or its absence within the context of history and political realities. "And that will have to do until someone else comes in a burst of song, color, and laughter to conquer the last refuge of the sacred, still inaccessibly hidden" (Kristeva 1980, 158).

Afterword

> When "The Repressed" of their culture and their society come back, it is an explosive return, which is *absolutely* shattering, staggering, overturning, with a force never let loose before.
> —Cixous and Clément, *The Newly Born Woman*

Finally, Morrison's texts represent this kind of "shattering" and "explosive" return, for through her language (most particularly through her language), she speaks what is unspeakable for mainstream discourse: the juxtaposition of woman and collective history, the dissolution of boundaries between sign and historical event, the unification of myth and cultural codes, the reinscription of meaning itself through a rendering of identification and desire. She *does* write the feminine text; she *does* compose a literature that is distinctly African American; her works *do* constitute a contribution to postmodernism; she *is* a deconstructionist. Or, she is none of these things because she is *all* of them—and more. She writes in the *difference*, in the spaces and the margins, from the vantage of otherness which then becomes the familiar.

The foregoing study has stressed this difference, a difference by which Morrison also defines her own text: "I am not *like* James Joyce; I am not *like* Thomas Hardy; I am not *like* Faulkner. I am not *like* in that sense" (McKay 1988, 1). As we have also seen, Morrison's novels defy those critical straitjackets which seek to analyze and define strictly within the contexts of either Freud or Marx, psychoanalysis or politics, although her works are always political, always concerned with class distinctions, and always profoundly psychoanalytic. Morrison is clearly outside of traditional dominant cultural inscriptions, but she does not create in a vacuum. She is, of course, not the first writer to stress the diffusion of the text as well as of identity, nor the first to articulate female desire, nor the first to reinscribe history. Nor is she exempt from the context of contemporary critical theory, particularly French feminist theory, which also seeks to break down oppositions and hierarchies, to diffuse modalities, and reinscribe identity and desire. However, Morrison is greater than the terms employed to define her. She represents the *extreme* of that which critical theory has conceptualized, taking theory itself to the edge of the abyss, to a point beyond meaning, to signification that is truly "unspeakable."

Thus Morrison's texts are prophetic in many ways, another of which is that they give voice to a cultural rupture which has already occurred and is now being documented by a great deal of critical attention and literary analysis. In light of the tremendous impact of Morrison's fictions and those of other contemporary women writers (and particularly African American women writers), arguments about canonicity that have preoccupied scholars in the recent past seem already anachronistic, for the sanctity of the canon is already threatened, demasculinized if not actually feminized.

Appropriately, Morrison has spoken on revolutionizing the Western literary canon and defined it in its political context:

> Canon building is Empire building. Canon defense is national defense. Canon debate, whatever the terrain, nature, and range (of criticism, of history, or the history of knowledge, of the definition of language, the universality of aesthetic principles, the sociology of art, the humanistic imagination), is the clash of cultures. And *all* of the interests are vested. (1990, 207)

Changes in the humanistic status quo, Morrison indicates, are not so much historical events, temporal and physical processes, as mental structures, new ways of seeing even the history that has informed and dictated culture. She would not wish, she has said, the destruction or the elimination of that which comprises the canon: "And, I, at least, do not intend to live without Aeschylus or William Shakespeare, or James or Twain or Hawthorne, or Melville, etc., etc., etc." Rather, it is canonicity itself, the sanctity and the political conservatism that sanctity represents, which Morrison would eliminate: "There must be some way to enhance canon readings without enshrining them" (1990, 204–5).

Morrison's fictions are foremost among those which challenge the institutions that are indifferent to difference and intent on preserving a myth of a homogeneous tradition for its own sake and for its political ramifications. Canon-building has been accomplished by scholars who universalized texts by ignoring the cultural specificities that differentiated them and who insisted on totalizing concepts of gender, race, and subjectivity. The very concept of canonicity is subverted by writers like Morrison who represent language as difference rather than as unified or cohesive discourse, and who also represent more accurately the plurality of the American heritage, including that of the African American woman writer. Morrison's work both poses and represents the intellectual crisis that will surely engage readers and critics for the next generation.

Notes

Introduction

1. For an analysis of the specific relevance of the term "conjure" in African American discourse, see Marjorie Pryse and Hortense Spillers, eds., *Conjuring: Black Women, Fiction, and Literary Tradition*.
2. According to Showalter: "We can think of the "wild zone" of women's culture spatially, experientially, or metaphysically. Spatially it stands for an area which is literally no-man's land, a place forbidden to men. . . . Experientially it stands for the aspects of the female lifestyle which are outside of or unlike those of men; again, there is no corresponding zone of male experience alien to women. But, if we think of the wild zone metaphysically, or in terms of consciousness, it has no corresponding male space since all of male consciousness is within the circle of the dominant structure and is thus accessible to or structured by language. In this sense, the "wild" is always imaginary; from the male point of view, it may simply be the projection of the unconscious. In terms of cultural anthropology, women know what the male crescent is like, even if they have never seen it, because it becomes the subject of legend (like the wilderness). But men do not know what is in the wild" (1985, 262).

Chapter 1

1. Morrison writes, in "Unspeakable Things Unspoken: The Afro-American Presence in American Literature," that what most concerns her in *The Bluest Eye* is "the silence at its center. The void that is Pecola's 'unbeing'" (220).
2. Keith E. Byerman argues that Son's destiny is more heroic: "He does not go back to the womb, as Jadine thought, but into the domain of the true black man" (84).
3. Freud's analogy of the preoedipal phase with archaeology might well

109

link with Milkman's archaeological quest in *Song of Solomon* and with Pilate's directions to the cave. Both the cave and the field of archaeology, in essence, are areas of privileged femininity.

4. Showalter writes, in "Feminist Criticism in the Wilderness": "For some feminist critics, the wild zone, or "female space," must be the address of a genuinely women-centered criticism, theory, and art, whose shared project is to bring into being the symbolic weight of female consciousness, to make the invisible visible, to make the silent speak" (263).

5. Mae Gwendolyn Henderson defines "speaking in tongues" as the "ability to speak in and through the spirit. Associated with glossolalia—speech in unknown tongues—it is ecstatic, rapturous, inspired speech based on a relation of intimacy and identification between the individual and God" (23).

6. According to Marianne Hirsch, silence is a form of discourse between all mothers and daughters, and, particularly in *Sula*, there is much that "remains unspeakable and indeed unspoken. A focus on this mother/daughter plot may suggest a particular form of the postmodern, deeply rooted in racial history, feminist consciousness, and political engagement."

7. Susan Gubar, in "The Blank Page," sees absence, blankness, as "a mysterious but potent act of resistance" (305) and as "a sacred space consecrated to female creativity" (307).

8. In a public lecture in Columbus, Ohio, in 1988, Morrison responded to a question about the stylistic shifts in *Beloved* by stating that they represented "writer's block," that the world she had created was so painful to her that at times she found that world impossible to reenter.

9. We shall also see in Chapter 3 that history itself partakes of a dreamscape or a nightmare, and that, again, boundaries between reality and fantasy are confused.

Chapter 2

1. Susan Willis writes in "I Shop Therefore I Am" that Hagar has destroyed herself through her own and Milkman's rejection of blackness: Hagar "decides that in order to hold on to her boyfriend she must make herself into a less-black woman. What Hagar does not grasp is that Milkman's uncaring regard for her is an expression of his primary sexism as well as his internalized acceptance of the larger society's racist measure of blacks in terms of how closely an individual's skin and hair approximate the white model" (1989, 178).

2. In an interview with Claudia Tate, for example, Morrison stated, "I don't use much autobiography in my writing. My life is uneventful. Writing has to do with the imagination. It's being able to open a door or think the unthinkable, no matter how silly it may appear" (1989, 127).

3. Nellie Y. McKay quotes Morrison as saying, "No author tells these stories. They are just told—meanderingly—as though they are going in several directions at the same time" (1983, 417).

4. See the discussion in Chapter 1 of blackness as invisibility and absence in *The Bluest Eye*.

5. In *Beloved*, whiteness rather than blackness becomes the signifier for absence, as Beloved recalls the slavers in the Middle Passage as "men without skin" (212).

6. Henderson argues that Sula's mark indicates as much about the sexism inherent in the black community as it does about her own identity: "Sula is marked from birth. Hers is a mark of nativity—a biological rather than a cultural inscription, appropriate in this instance because it functions to mark her as a 'naturally' inferior female within the black community" (27).

7. Roberta Rubenstein interprets the significance of marking quite differently. She writes, in *Boundaries of the Self*, "Whether self-created, imposed by others, or dictated by accident, each of the representations of physical or psychic mutilations or incompleteness expresses the characters' inner distress and social or cultural plight" (233).

8. As Trudier Harris has written in "Reconnecting Fragments: Afro-American Folk Tradition in *The Bluest Eye*," "To be called 'out of one's name' . . . can be just as negatively powerful as a nickname can be positive" (1988, 72).

9. It is interesting that Margaret Street enjoys romanticizing Jadine's blackness, at one point insisting on a comparison with Eurydice of the film *Black Orpheus*. Jadine resists: "She was uncomfortable with the way Margaret stirred her into blackening up or universaling out, always alluding to or ferreting out what she believed were racial characteristics" (54). Morrison implies, however, that Jadine's resistance indicates a problem with her own self-image as well as with Margaret's patronizing perceptions.

10. In an interview with Sandi Russell, Morrison commented on the strong ties among the women of her family: "I remember my grandmother and my great-grandmother. I had to answer to those women, had to know that whatever I did was easy in comparison with what they had to go through. . . . They taught me how to dream" (45).

11. Marianne Hirsch also explores ideas of subjectivity in *Beloved*:

"When Sethe tentatively says, at the end of the novel, 'Me? Me?', she begins for the first time to speak *for herself*. However, she can do so only in the context of another human bond; she can do so only because Paul D is holding her hand." Hirsch concludes that this represents "an affirmation of subjectivity which, even when it is maternal, can only emerge in and through human interconnection" (198).

12. Morrison's recurring image in this novel of the single eye—recall the reference quoted earlier in this chapter to women without men as "sour-tipped needles featuring one constant empty eye" (105)—may be associated with the fairy tale about the three sisters, One-Eye, Two-Eye, and Three-Eye.

13. According to Reddy in "The Tripled Plot and Center of *Sula*," Sula's "wish to be Nel is what drives Sula into her sexual experimentation with Jude" (37).

14. The single exception to this rule in Morrison's novels is the relationships that exist among the men at Sweet Home in *Beloved* and among the convicts in Alfred, Georgia, who are literally chained together and mutually dependent for survival itself. Perhaps the element of common victimization is the basis of the respect, even brotherhood, which characterizes these relationships.

15. Morrison states, in "The Afro-American Presence in American Literature," that she perceives the Tar Baby folktale to which her novel refers as being about masks: "Not masks as covering what is to be hidden, but how masks come to life, take life over, exercise the tensions between itself and what it covers. For Son, the most effective mask is none. For the others the construction is careful and delicately borne, but the masks they make have a life of their own and collide with those they come in contact with" (1990, 227).

Chapter 3

1. Morrison suggests a comparison of Jadine's and Son's relationship to the classic myth of Orpheus and Eurydice in that conversation early in the novel when Margaret and Jadine discuss the film *Black Orpheus*. Margaret comments on the beauty of Eurydice's hair, but Jadine subverts the implied romantic notion of race by interpreting the reference as being to the hair in Eurydice's armpits (54). Nevertheless, the allusion is relevant: Son unsuccessfully attempts to rescue his Eurydice from the hell that is her white-world identification.

2. Morrison has also commented: "There's a notion out in the land that there are human beings one writes about, and then there are black people or Indians or some other marginal group. If you write

about the world from that point of view, somehow it is considered lesser. It's racist, of course. The fact that I chose to write about black people means I've been stimulated to write about black people. We are people, not aliens. We live, we love, and we die. . . . Insensitive white people cannot deal with black writing, but then they cannot deal with their own literature either" (Tate 1989, 121).

Chapter 4

1. Hélène Cixous describes the orange as a symbol of female sexuality and also as an image of the perfect zero in *Vivre l'orange*.
2. As Deborah E. McDowell notes in her excellent article on "'The Self and Other': Reading Toni Morrison's *Sula* and the Black Female Text," "Jelly and pudding are metaphors of sexuality characteristic in classic blues lyrics" (1988, 82).
3. McDowell, for one, disagrees with such an assessment of any such agenda as castration in the works of black women writers: "What lies behind this smoke screen is an unacknowledged jostling for space in the literary marketplace . . ." (1989, 83).
4. Smith writes: "Despite the apparent heterosexuality of the female characters I discovered in re-reading *Sula* that it works as a lesbian novel not only because of the passionate friendship between Sula and Nel, but because of Morrison's consistently critical stance toward the heterosexual institutions of male/female relationships, marriage, and the family. Consciously or not, Morrison's work poses both lesbian and feminist questions about Black women's autonomy and their impact upon each other's lives" (165).
5. Theodore O. Mason, Jr., comments on the number of critics who object to just such patterns in Morrison's fictions and claim that she "unnecessarily problematizes Afro-American cultural patterns by representing them as anarchic and frequently violent" (173). Valerie Smith's concern, one that I feel sure is shared by Morrison, is that the symbolic and imagistic "return to earth" is a dangerous precedent for women: "This association of black women with reembodiment resembles rather closely the association, in classic Western philosophy and in nineteenth-century cultural constructions of womanhood, of women of color with the body and therefore with animal passions and slave labor" (45).
6. Jane Bakerman, in "Failures of Love: Female Initiation in the Novels of Toni Morrison," argues that First Corinthians is the only woman in *Song of Solomon* who has "a chance for even modified happiness" (563).

Bibliography

Primary Sources

Beloved. New York: Knopf, 1987.
The Black Book. Comp. Middleton Harris, ed. Toni Morrison. New York: Random House, 1974.
The Bluest Eye. New York: Pocket Books, 1970.
Song of Solomon. New York: Signet, 1978.
Sula. New York: Bantam, 1975.
Tar Baby. New York: Signet, 1981.
"Unspeakable Things Unspoken: The Afro-American Presence in American Literature." In *Modern Critical Views: Toni Morrison*, ed. Harold Bloom, 201–30. New York: Chelsea House, 1990.

Secondary Sources

Adams, Hazard, and Leroy Searle, eds. *Critical Theory since 1965*. Tallahassee: Florida State University Press, 1986.
Awkward, Michael. "Appropriative Gestures: Theory and Afro-American Literary Criticism." In *Gender and Theory: Dialogues on Feminist Criticism*, ed. Linda Kauffman, 238–45. New York: Basil Blackwell, 1989.
————. "Roadblocks and Relatives: Critical Revision in Toni Morrison's *The Bluest Eye*." In *Critical Essays on Toni Morrison*, ed. Nellie Y. McKay, 57–67. Boston: G. K. Hall, 1988.
Baker, Houston A., Jr. "When Lindbergh Sleeps with Bessie Smith: The Writing of Place in Toni Morrison's *Sula*." In *The Difference Within: Feminism and Critical Theory*, ed. Elizabeth Meese and Alice Parker, 85–113. Philadelphia: John Benjamin's Publishing Company, 1989.
Bakerman, Jane S. "Failures of Love: Female Initiation in the Novels of Toni Morrison." *American Literature* 52 (1981): 541–63.
Banyiwa-Horne, Naana. "The Scary Face of the Self: An Analysis of

115

the Character of Sula in Toni Morrison's *Sula*." *Sage* 2 (1985): 28–31.

Barksdale, Richard K. "Castration Symbolism in Recent Black American Fiction." *College Language Association Journal* 29, no. 4 (June 1986): 400–413.

Bell, Roseann, Bettye Parker, and Beverly Guy-Shiftall, eds. *Sturdy Black Bridges: Visions of Black Women in Literature*. New York: Doubleday, 1979.

Berg, Temma F., Anna Shannon Elfenbein, Jeanne Larsen, and Eliza Kay Spacks, eds. *Engendering The Word: Feminist Essays in Psychosexual Poetics*. Urbana: University of Illinois Press, 1989.

———. "Suppressing the Language of Wo(man): The Dream as a Common Language." In *Engendering The Word*, ed. Berg et al., 3–28. Urbana: University of Illinois Press, 1989.

Blau du Plessis, Rachael. *Writing Beyond the Ending: Narrative Strategies of Twentieth-Century Women Writers*. Bloomington: Indiana University Press, 1986.

Bloom, Harold, ed. *Modern Critical Views: Toni Morrison*. New York: Chelsea House, 1990.

Brenner, Gerry. "*Song of Solomon*: Morrison's Rejection of Rank's Monomyth and Feminism." In *Critical Essays on Toni Morrison*, ed. Nellie Y. McKay, 114–24. Boston: G. K. Hall, 1988.

Butler, Judith. *Gender Trouble: Feminism and the Subversion of Identity*. New York: Routledge, 1990.

Byerman, Keith E. "Beyond Realism: The Fictions of Toni Morrison." In *Modern Critical Views: Toni Morrison*, ed. Bloom, 55–84. New York: Chelsea House, 1990.

———. *Fingering the Jagged Edge: Tradition and Form in Recent Black Fiction*. Athens: University of Georgia Press, 1985.

Campbell, Jane. *Mythic Black Fiction: The Transformation of History*. Knoxville: University of Tennessee Press, 1986.

Chodorow, Nancy J. *Feminism and Psychoanalytic Theory*. New Haven: Yale University Press, 1989.

———. *The Reproduction of Mothering: Psychoanalysis and the Sociology of Gender*. Berkeley: University of California Press, 1978.

Christian, Barbara. *Black Feminist Criticism: Perspectives on Black Women Writers*. New York: Pergamon Press, 1985.

———. *Black Women Novelists: The Development of a Tradition, 1892– 1976*. Westport, Ct.: Greenwood Press, 1980.

———. "But What Do We Think We're Doing Anyway: The State of Black Feminist Criticism(s), or My Version of a Little Bit of History." In *Changing Our Own Words: Essays on Criticism, Theory, and Writing by Black Women*, Cheryl A. Wall, ed., 58–74. New Brunswick: Rutgers University Press, 1989.

———. "Community and Nature in the Novels of Toni Morrison." *Journal of Ethnic Studies* 7 (Winter 1980): 64–78.

———. "The Race for Theory." *Feminist Studies* 14, no. 1 (Spring 1988): 67–79.

Cixous, Hélène. "Castration or Decapitation?" trans. Annette Kuhn. *Signs* 7, no. 11 (Autumn 1981): 41–55.

———. "The Laugh of the Medusa." In *Critical Theory since 1965*, ed. Adams and Searle, 309–20. Tallahassee: Florida State University Press, 1986.

———. *Vivre l'orange*. Paris: Editions des femmes, 1980.

———, and Catherine Clément. *The Newly Born Woman*, trans. Betsy Wing. Minneapolis: University of Minnesota Press, 1986.

Davis, Cynthia A. "Self, Society, and Myth in Toni Morrison's Fiction." In *Modern Critical Views: Toni Morrison*, ed. Bloom, 7–26. New York: Chelsea House, 1990.

de Lauretis, Teresa, ed. *Feminist Studies/Critical Studies*. Bloomington: Indiana University Press, 1986.

Denard, Carolyn. "The Convergence of Feminism and Ethnicity in the Fiction of Toni Morrison." In *Critical Essays on Toni Morrison*, ed. McKay, 171–78. Boston: G. K. Hall, 1988.

de Weever, Jacqueline. "Toni Morrison's Use of Fairy Tale, Folk Tale, and Myth in *Song of Solomon*." *Southern Folklore Quarterly* 44 (1980): 131–44.

Dixon, Melvin. "Like an Eagle in the Air: Toni Morrison." In *Modern Critical Views: Toni Morrison*, ed. Bloom, 115–42. New York: Chelsea House, 1990.

Donovan, Josephine. *Feminist Literary Criticism: Explorations in Theory*. Louisville: University of Kentucky Press, 1989.

Epstein, Grace. "An Interview with Toni Morrison." *Ohio Journal* 9, no. 3 (Spring 1986): 3–8.

———. "Fluid Bodies: Female Narrative Desire and Layering in the Novels of Morrison, Lessing, and Atwood." PhD. diss., The Ohio State University, 1991.

Evans, Mari, ed. *Black Women Writers: 1950–1980, A Critical Evaluation*. New York: Doubleday, 1984.

Fabre, Genevieve. "Genealogical Archaeology or the Quest for Legacy in Toni Morrison's *Song of Solomon*." In *Critical Essays on Toni Morrison*, ed. McKay, 105–13. Boston: G .K. Hall, 1988.

Fisher, Dexter, ed. *The Third Woman: Minority Women Writers of the United States*. Boston: Houghton Mifflin, 1980.

Gallop, Jane. *The Daughter's Seduction*. Ithaca, N.Y.: Cornell University Press, 1982.

Gates, Henry Louis, Jr., ed. *Black Literature and Literary Theory*. New York: Metheun, 1984.

————. *Figures in Black: Words, Signs, and the "Racial" Self.* New York: Oxford University Press, 1987.

————, ed. *"Race," Writing, and Difference.* Chicago: University of Chicago Press, 1986.

————. *The Signifying Monkey: A Theory of Afro-American Literary Criticism.* New York: Oxford University Press, 1988.

Gelfand, Elissa D., and Virginia Thorndike Hulls. *French Feminist Criticism: Women, Language and Literature.* New York: Garland, 1984.

Giddings, Paula. *When and Where I Enter: The Impact of Black Women on Race and Sex in America.* New York: Bantam, 1984.

Grant, Robert. "Absence into Presence: The Semantics of Memory and 'Missing' Subjects in Toni Morrison's *Sula.*" In *Critical Essays on Toni Morrison,* ed. McKay, 90–104. Boston: G. K. Hall, 1988.

Grosz, Elisabeth. *Sexual Subversions: Three French Feminists.* Sydney: Allen and Unwin, 1989.

Gubar, Susan. "The Blank Page." In *The New Feminist Criticism,* ed. Elaine Showalter, 243–70. New York: Pantheon, 1985.

Harris, Trudier. *Exorcising Blackness: Historical and Literary Lynching and Burning Rituals.* Bloomington: Indiana University Press, 1984.

————. "Reconnecting Fragments: Afro-American Folk Tradition in *The Bluest Eye.*" In *Critical Essays on Toni Morrison,* ed. McKay, 68–76. Boston: G. K. Hall, 1988.

Henderson, Mae Gwendolyn. "Speaking in Tongues: Dialogics, Dialectics, and the Black Woman Writer's Literary Tradition." In *Changing Our Own Words: Essays on Criticism, Theory, and Writing by Black Women,* ed. Wall, 16–37. New Brunswick: Rutgers University Press, 1989.

Hernton, Calvin C. *The Sexual Mountain and Black Women Writers.* New York: Doubleday, 1987.

Hirsch, Marianne. *The Mother/Daughter Plot: Narrative, Psychoanalysis, Feminism.* Bloomington: Indiana University Press, 1989.

Holloway, Karla F. C., and Stephane Demetrakopoulos. *New Dimensions of Spirituality: A Biracial and Bicultural Reading of the Novels of Toni Morrison.* New York: Greenwood Press, 1987.

House, Elizabeth B. "Artists and the Art of Living: Order and Disorder in Toni Morrison's Fiction." *Modern Fiction Studies* 34 (1988): 27–44.

Hull, Gloria T., Patricia Bell Scott, and Barbara Smith, eds. *All the Women Are White, All the Blacks Are Men, But Some of Us Are Brave: Black Women's Studies.* Old Westbury, N.Y.: Feminist Press, 1982.

Irigaray, Luce. *This Sex Which Is Not One,* trans. Catherine Porter. Ithaca, N.Y.: Cornell University Press, 1985.

————. *The Speculum of the Other Woman,* trans. Gillian C. Gill. Ithaca, N.Y.: Cornell University Press, 1985.

Jardine, Alice, and Hester Eisenstein, eds. *The Future of Difference: The Scholar and the Feminist*. Boston: G. K. Hall, 1980.

———. "Gynesis." In *Critical Theory since 1965*, ed. Adams and Searle, 559–70. Tallahassee: Florida State University Press, 1986.

———. *Gynesis*. Ithaca, N.Y.: Cornell University Press, 1985.

Jones, Ann Rosalind. "Writing the Body: Toward an Understanding of *l'Ecriture feminine*." In *The New Feminist Criticism*, ed. Showalter, 361–78. New York: Pantheon, 1985.

Jones, Bessie W., and Audrey L. Vinson. *The World of Toni Morrison*. Dubuque: Kendall/Hunt, 1985.

Joseph, Gloria I., and Jill Lewis. *Common Differences: Conflicts in Black and White Feminist Perspectives*. New York: Doubleday, 1981.

Joyce, Joyce A. "The Black Canon: Reconstructing Black American Literary Criticism." *New Literary History* 18, no. 2 (1987): 335–44.

Kauffman, Linda, ed. *Gender and Theory: Dialogues on Feminist Criticism*. New York: Basil Blackwell, 1989.

Keohane, Nannerl O., Michelle Z. Rosaldo, and Barbara C. Gelpi, eds. *Feminist Theory: A Critique of Ideology*. Chicago: University of Chicago Press, 1982.

Kessler-Harris, Alice, and William McBrien. *Faith of a (Woman) Writer*. Westport, Conn.: Greenwood Press, 1988.

Kristeva, Julia. *About Chinese Women*, trans. Anita Barrows. London: M. Eoyers, 1977.

———. *Desire in Language: A Semiotic Approach to Literature and Art*, ed. Leon S. Roudiez, trans. Thomas Goza, Alice Jardine, and Leon Roudiez. New York: Columbia University Press, 1980.

———. *Polylogue*. Paris: Editions du Seuil, 1977.

———. "Women's Time," trans. Alice Jardine. *Signs* 7, no. 1 (Autumn 1981): 13–35.

Le Clair, Thomas. "'The Language Must Not Sweat': A Conversation with Toni Morrison." *New Republic* (March 1981): 21–29.

Lester, Rosemarie K. "An Interview with Toni Morrison: Hessian Radio Network, Frankfurt, W. Germany." In *Critical Essays on Toni Morrison*, ed. McKay, 47–54. Boston: G. K. Hall, 1988.

Lifton, Robert Jay. *The Life of the Self: Toward a New Psychology*. New York: Simon and Schuster, 1976.

Marks, Elaine, and Isabelle de Courtivron, eds. *New French Feminisms: An Anthology*. Amherst: University of Massachusetts Press, 1980.

Mason, Theodore O., Jr. "The Novelist as Conservator: Stories and Comprehension in Toni Morrison's *Song of Solomon*." In *Modern Critical Views: Toni Morrison*, ed. Bloom, 171–88. New York: Chelsea House, 1990.

McConnell-Ginet, Sally, Ruth Borker, and Nelly Furman, eds. *Women and Language in Literature and Society*. New York: Praeger, 1980.

McDowell, Deborah E. "New Directions for Black Feminist Criticism."
In *The New Feminist Criticism*, ed. Showalter, 186–99. New York:
Pantheon, 1985.

———. "Reading Family Matters." In *Changing Our Own Words: Essays
on Critical Theory and Writing by Black Women*, ed. Wall, 75–97.
New Brunswick, N.J.: Rutgers University Press, 1989.

———. "'The Self and the Other': Reading Toni Morrison's *Sula* and
the Black Female Text." In *Critical Essays on Toni Morrison*, ed. Mc-
Kay, 77–89. Boston: G. K. Hall, 1988.

McKay, Nellie Y., ed. *Critical Essays on Toni Morrison*. Boston: G. K. Hall,
1988.

Meese, Elizabeth, and Alice Parker, eds. *The Difference Within: Feminism
and Critical Theory*. Philadelphia: John Benjamin's Publishing Company, 1989.

Middleton, David L. *Toni Morrison: An Annotated Bibliography*. New
York: Garland, 1987.

Miner, Madonne M. "Lady No Longer Sings the Blues: Rape, Madness,
and Silence in *The Bluest Eye*." In *Modern Critical Views: Toni Morrison*, ed. Bloom, 85–100. New York: Chelsea House, 1990.

Mobley, Marilyn Sanders. "A Different Remembering: Memory, History
and Meaning in Toni Morrison's *Beloved*." In *Modern Critical Views:
Toni Morrison*, ed. Bloom, 85–100. New York: Chelsea House,
1990.

Moi, Toril, ed. *The Kristeva Reader*. New York: Columbia University
Press, 1986.

———. *Sexual/Textual Politics: Feminist Literary Theory*. New York: Methuen, 1985.

Newton, Judith, and Deborah Rosenfelt, eds. *Feminist Criticism and Social Change: Sex, Class and Race in Literature and Culture*. New
York: Methuen, 1985.

Nicholson, Linda J., ed. *Feminism/Postmodernism*. New York: Routledge,
1990.

O'Shaughnessy, Kathleen. "'Life life life life': The Community as Chorus
in *Song of Solomon*." In *Critical Essays on Toni Morrison*, ed. McKay,
125–34. Boston: G. K. Hall, 1988.

Otten, Terry. *The Crime of Innocence in the Fiction of Toni Morrison*. Columbia: University of Missouri Press, 1989.

———. "The Crime of Innocence in Toni Morrison's *Tar Baby*." In *Modern Critical Views: Toni Morrison*, ed. Bloom, 101–14. New York:
Chelsea House, 1990.

Pateman, Carol, and Elizabeth Gross. *Feminist Challenges: Social and Political Theory*. Boston: Northeastern University Press, 1986.

Pryse, Marjorie, and Hortense J. Spillers, eds. *Conjuring: Black Women,*

Fiction, and Literary Tradition. Bloomington: Indiana University Press, 1985.

Rainwater, Catherine, and William J. Scheick, eds. *Contemporary American Women Writers: Narrative Strategies.* Lexington: University Press of Kentucky, 1985.

Reddy, Maurine T. "The Tripled Plot and Center of Sula." *Black American Literature Forum* 22, no. 1 (Spring 1988): 29–45.

Rich, Adrienne. *On Lies, Secrets, and Silence: Selected Prose 1966–1978.* New York: Norton, 1979.

———. "Compulsory Heterosexuality and Lesbian Existence." *Signs* 5, no. 4 (1980): 212–41.

Rigney, Barbara Hill. *Lilith's Daughters: Women and Religion in Contemporary Fiction.* Madison: University of Wisconsin Press, 1982.

Rubenstein, Roberta. *Boundaries of the Self: Gender, Culture, Fiction.* Urbana: University of Illinois Press, 1987.

Russel, Sandi. "Conversation from Abroad." In *Critical Essays on Toni Morrison*, ed. McKay, 45–47. Boston: G. K. Hall, 1988.

Samuels, Wilfred D., and Clenora Hudson-Weems. *Toni Morrison.* Boston: Twayne Publishers, 1990.

Sargent, Robert. "A Way of Ordering Experience: A Study of Toni Morrison's *The Bluest Eye* and *Sula.*" In *Faith of a (Woman) Writer*, ed. Alice Kessler-Harris and William McBrien. Westport, Conn.: Greenwood Press, 1988.

Scruggs, Charles. "The Nature of Desire in Toni Morrison's *Song of Solomon.*" *Arizona Quarterly* 38 (1982): 311–35.

Shannon, Anna. "'We Was Girls Together': A Study of Toni Morrison's *Sula.*" *Midwestern Miscellany* 10 (1982): 9–22.

Showalter, Elaine. "Feminist Criticism in the Wilderness." In *The New Feminist Criticism*, ed. Showalter, 243–70. New York: Pantheon, 1985.

———, ed. *The New Feminist Criticism: Essays on Women, Literature, and Society.* New York: Pantheon, 1985.

Smith, Barbara, ed. *Home Girls: A Black Feminist Anthology.* Watertown, Mass.: Persephone Press, 1983.

———. "Toward a Black Feminist Criticism." In *The New Feminist Criticism*, ed. Showalter, 168–85. New York: Pantheon, 1985.

Smith, Valerie. "Black Feminist Theory and the Representation of the 'Other.'" In *Changing Our Own Words: Essays on Criticism, Theory, and Writing by Black Women*, ed. Wall, 38–57. New Brunswick, N.J.: Rutgers University Press, 1989.

Spiller, Hortense J. "A Hateful Passion, A Lost Love." In *Modern Critical Views: Toni Morrison*, ed. Bloom, 27–54. New York: Chelsea House, 1990.

Spivak, Gayatri Chakravorty. "A Response to *The Difference Within*." In *The Difference Within: Feminism and Critical Theory*, ed. Meese and Parker, 207–18. Philadelphia: John Benjamin's Publishing Company, 1989.

Stein, Karen F. "Toni Morrison's *Sula*: A Black Woman's Epic." *Black American Literature Forum* 18, no. 4 (Winter 1984): 146–50.

Stepto, Robert B., and Michael S. Harper, eds. *Chant of Saints: A Gathering of Afro-American Literature, Art, and Scholarship*. Urbana: University of Illinois Press, 1979.

———. *From Behind the Veil: A Study of Afro-American Narrative*. Urbana: University of Illinois Press, 1979.

———. "'Intimate Things in Place': A Conversation with Toni Morrison." In *Chant of Saints*, ed. Stepto and Harper, 213–29. Urbana: University of Illinois Press, 1979.

Tate, Claudia. "On Black Literary Women and the Evolution of Critical Discourse." *Tulsa Studies in Women's Literature* 5 (1986): 111–23.

———. *Black Women Writers at Work*. New York: Continuum, 1989.

Todd, Janet, ed. *Gender and Literary Voice*. New York: Holmes and Meier, 1988.

Traylor, Eleanor W. "The Fabulous World of Toni Morrison: *Tar Baby*." In *Critical Essays on Toni Morrison*, ed. McKay, 135–49. Boston: G. K. Hall, 1988.

Wagner, Linda J. "Toni Morrison: Mastery of Narrative." In *Contemporary American Women Writers: Narrative Strategies*, ed. Rainwater and Scheick, 191–205. Lexington: University of Kentucky Press, 1985.

Wall, Cheryl A., ed. *Changing Our Own Words: Essays on Criticism, Theory, and Writing by Black Women*. New Brunswick, N.J.: Rutgers University Press, 1989.

Washington, Mary Helen. *Invented Lives: Narratives of Black Women, 1860–1960*. New York: Doubleday, 1987.

Waugh, Patricia. *Feminine Fictions: Revising the Postmodern*. New York: Routledge, 1989.

Weixlmann, Joe, and Houston A. Baker, Jr., eds. *Black Feminist Criticism and Critical Theory*. Greenwood, Fla.: Fenkevill, 1988.

Werner, Craig H. "The Briar Patch as Modernist Myth: Morrison, Barthes, and Tar Baby As-Is." In *Critical Essays on Toni Morrison*, ed. McKay, 150–70. Boston: G. K. Hall, 1988.

Willis, Susan. "Eruptions of Funk: Historicizing Toni Morrison." *Black American Literature Forum* 16 (1982): 34–42.

———. "I Shop Therefore I Am: Is There a Place for Afro-American Culture in Commodity Culture?" In *Changing Our Own Words*, ed. Wall, 173–95. New Brunswick, N.J.: Rutgers University Press, 1989.

————. *Specifying: Black Women Writing the American Experience*. Madison: University of Wisconsin Press, 1987.

Wittig, Monique. *Les Guérillères*, trans. Peter Owen. New York: Avon, 1971.

Winnett, Susan. "Coming Unstrung: Women, Men, Narrative, and Principles of Pleasure." *PMLA* 105, no. 3 (May 1990): 505–18.

Yaeger, Patricia. *Honey-Mad Women: Emancipatory Strategies in Women's Fiction*. New York: Columbia University Press, 1988.

————. "Toward a Female Sublime." In *Gender and Theory: Dialogues on Feminist Criticism*, ed. Kaufman. New York: Basil Blackwell, 1989.

Index

125